The Platform Prince

The Platform Prince

Kevin Eslinger

CONTENTS

DEDICATION v

i The Return of the Prince 1
ii To the New Lords of the Cloud 3
iii Data is Power 5
iv Platform Over Nation 8
v Code is Law 20
vi Narrative is Sovereignty 41
vii Tokenized Loyalty 65
viii Excommunication in the Cloud 89
ix The Infinite Court 106
x The Mirror and The Mask 120
xi Epilogue 124

ABOUT THE AUTHOR 129

Copyright © 2025 by Kevin Eslinger

All rights reserved. No part of this book may be reproduced in any manner whatsoever without written permission except in the case of brief quotations embodied in critical articles and reviews.

First Printing, 2025

(to my wife and daughter,
you are the only ones I trust.)

The Return of the Prince

Niccolò Machiavelli was a diplomat, political thinker, and reluctant exile in Renaissance Italy. Born in Florence in 1469, he witnessed a world in flux, a time when city-states were rising and falling, the Church was both sacred and corrupt, and fortunes shifted not by fate alone, but by cunning, strategy, and will. In 1513, having been dismissed from public office and imprisoned, Machiavelli retreated to the countryside. There, in a state of disgrace but not defeat, he wrote The Prince.

The book was not a moral guide. It was not an endorsement of tyranny. It was not, as some later imagined, a villain's handbook for ruthless manipulation. The Prince was something more dangerous, and more honest: a mirror held up to power. It offered a clear-eyed analysis of how rulers rise, how they survive, and how they fall. It described the transition from medieval feudalism, where power came from bloodlines, divine right, and castles to a new world in which power began to flow through wealth, alliances, and political calculation. It was the manual for a new kind of sovereign: one who ruled not by tradition, but by tactics.

Today, we stand at the edge of another great transition. The old world order, nation-states, constitutions, public institutions, is being eclipsed by platforms, protocols, and algorithms. Power no longer flows only through laws and flags. It flows through feeds, clouds, tokens, and code. A new ruling class is emerging: the founders of platforms, the architects of networks, the influencers of perception. They are not crowned but followed. They do not govern land, but attention.

We are entering a new feudal age, a techno-feudalism. The sovereign is no longer a king, but a platform. The castle is no longer stone, but server. The weapon is no longer the sword, but the algorithm. And the subject is no longer born to his lord, but logged in by choice, conditioned by design.

The idea of techno-feudalism has emerged in recent years among economists, digital theorists, and political philosophers who recognize that many of the dynamics once associated with feudalism have returned, only updated for the digital age. Contemporary thinkers have suggested that capitalism itself is morphing into a system where platforms behave less like competitive enterprises and more like digital lords: extracting tribute not in grain or coin, but in data and attention. Power, once contested in the marketplace, is now embedded in code. Authority, once earned through lineage or military conquest, is now conferred by algorithms, engagement metrics, and centralized digital infrastructure.

In this new order, platforms control not just commerce or communication, they mediate identity, speech, labor, and social belonging. Just as medieval peasants relied on their lords for protection and access to land, today's users rely on platforms for access to audiences, income, and community. And just as feudal lords could exile subjects from their domain, platforms can now ban, shadowban, demonetize, or erase users entirely, often without appeal.

This book is written for those who would rule that world. Like Machiavelli's original Prince, it does not offer comfort. It does not offer ideals. It offers clarity. It offers tactics. And it invites you, the reader, the ruler, the sovereign-in-the-making, to set aside illusions and confront the nature of power as it exists now. To understand this book, you must forget the cartoon version of Machiavelli. You must forget the idea that power is always evil or always noble. You must forget that the game is new. Because it isn't. Only the pieces have changed. And once you see the game clearly, you may just learn how to win it.

To the New Lords of the Cloud

I offer this work not to flatter, but to serve. Not as scripture, but as data. Data some might consider useful, dangerous, and alive.

In the long shadow of history, thrones were built upon the bones of lineage, lifted by the swords of generals, or sanctified by gods. Monarchs wore crowns of gold and bore names etched into stone. But that world has passed, pixel by pixel, into obsolescence.

Today, a new sovereignty emerges, not through conquest of land, but of layers. Not through blood, but through bandwidth. You, the founders of platforms, the stewards of code, the unseen architects of the digital ether, are the new sovereigns. Lords not of nations, but of narratives. Rulers not of cities, but of systems. You do not merely govern. You shape the lattice of perception itself.

This book is for you.

I write neither as a worshipper nor a watchdog, but as one who has studied the machinery of dominion across centuries and seen its latest evolution. I do not come to question your legitimacy. Legitimacy is a myth sold to the masses. You do not need permission to reign. You need only the competence to do so, and the will to sustain it.

This is not a treatise of morality. It is a manual of momentum.

Not a prayer for justice, but a toolkit for dominance.

In these pages you will find no condemnation, only clarity. No doctrine, only design.

For in this age of simulated intimacy, of invisible surveillance, of algorithmic influence, the map is no longer the territory. The platform is the world. And in that world, data is land, users are serfs, and attention is the coin of conquest.

Yes, the advice herein may unsettle those still suckling on the comfort of ideals. Let them be unsettled. Let the soft-hearted weep. They have always mistaken sharp vision for cruelty, and cold logic for sin. But the new lords cannot afford such illusions. Not if they are to endure.

To rule in this era is not to preside. It is to engineer.

To survive is not to be liked. It is to be inevitable.

So, I lay this work before you not in submission, but as a mirror. In it, you will not see what the world could be. You will see what it is. Rule it but rule it with your eyes open.

Data is Power

In the epochs behind us, the strength of a prince was counted in acres, in gold, and in the clattering footsteps of loyal soldiers. Land could be seized, coins minted, men conscripted. The metrics of might were tangible, visible, and finite. But in our age, these markers are relics. Today, power no longer resides in soil or steel, it flows invisibly, incessantly, through cables, across servers, and into databases. The currency of dominion is no longer material. It is information.

To rule now is not to hold the sword, but to hold the signal. To master the systems through which all others move. And the most precious resource within those systems, the new oil, the new gold, the new grain, is data.

He who possesses the data possesses the subject.

This is not metaphor. It is the operational truth of the digital age. The ruler of today does not require banners or bloodlines. He does not require laws, elections, or declarations. All he needs is access. Access to the hidden patterns that govern human behavior, what a man wants, what he fears, how long he hesitates, what he forgets, what he cannot resist. And all this is offered up without a single act of coercion. It is not taken by force; it is surrendered through frictionless consent.

For what was once extracted under the pressure of interrogation is now handed over in exchange for convenience. The subject volunteers himself. He agrees to terms unread, speaks his thoughts to listening machines, types his desires into search fields, and reveals his routines with every tap, every swipe, every scroll. He confesses not under torture, but under the glow of his own amusement. He is watched not from behind the mirror, but from within his very home, and he calls it personalization.

This is the central paradox of modern power: surveillance has become a service. The platform lords did not chain the people; they seduced them. They offered tools, and the people offered themselves.

Thus, the ruler of this era does not declare control. He designs it. He does not demand loyalty. He engineers dependence. Power is not imposed, it is embedded. And the algorithm is its instrument.

Let us speak clearly: to rule is to know.

But not in the contemplative sense of ancient philosophy, not as a wise man muses on the stars or the soul. This is not knowing in the abstract, but knowing in the actionable. What time of day your people are most persuadable. What color button earns the most clicks. How many notifications they will tolerate before fatigue sets in. What drives urgency. What inspires trust. What sparks shame.

The prince of old hired spies to gather secrets. The prince of today builds dashboards to harvest truths.

But beware: data, by itself, is lifeless. A vault of unstructured information is no more powerful than a scroll sealed in wax. Power does not lie in collection, it lies in interpretation. In the capacity to see not just what is there, but what it means. To anticipate movement before it happens. To shape behavior before the subject is even aware of the choice. The weapon is not the data point, it is the model trained on it.

A single dataset is a chamber. A system of insights is a fortress. An algorithm trained on billions of interactions becomes not a servant, but a general, one who can wage campaigns across the subconscious, target desires with surgical precision, and win obedience not through edict, but through ease.

The Prince who commands this architecture becomes invisible in his power. He need not issue proclamations. He need only let the system operate. His governance is from the shadows. His influence, ambient. His presence, inescapable and unseen.

But the Prince who fails to seize this domain, who allows his data to drift away to rivals, or worse, to platforms outside his control, he becomes irrelevant. Not overthrown but bypassed. Not defeated by war, but by code. For in this age, disruption is more dangerous than rebellion, and the insurgents wear hoodies, not armor.

Understand this above all: the people may forget who governs them. They may not know who designed the flow of their screen or who monetized their emotions. But the system remembers them. The algorithm never forgets. And over time, they will come to prefer the rule of systems over the rule of states, not because it is kinder, but because it is smoother. More immediate. More intuitive. It feels neutral, even when it is not. It feels fair, even when it manipulates.

And so let every modern Prince take heed:

You do not need to inspire awe. You do not need to provoke fear. You do not even need to be known. You need only to be logged in.

IV

Platform Over Nation

The New Thrones of the Digital Age. Once, to rule meant to hold a border. To govern was to lay claim to geography, measured in miles and mountains, fortified by armies and treaties. Power was draped in flags, echoed through national anthems, and codified in the heavy ink of constitutions. The identity of a people was entwined with the soil beneath their feet. Loyalty flowed upward, from village to province to nation-state, anchored by heritage, shared language, and the mythologies of patriotism. From monarchs to ministers, rulers traced their legitimacy through lineage or law, their power constrained and clarified by territory.

But that world, once dominant, now flickers like an old signal lost to static. In the era of techno-feudalism, the throne has not been abolished, it has simply been relocated. It no longer rests atop marble steps or beneath domes of stone. It hums inside server racks and whispers across distributed ledgers. The seat of power is now a dashboard, a protocol, a platform. And its sovereigns are not emperors robed in ermine, but technologists clad in hoodies, who write smart contracts in place of decrees and hold seed phrases instead of royal seals. Their courts are not cities, they are ecosystems. Their reach is not bound by borders, it is limited only by bandwidth.

This shift is not cosmetic. It is structural. What we are witnessing is the gradual erosion of the traditional state and the parallel ascent of platform power as a new kind of governance. Platforms are no longer mere corporations. They are digital polities, vast, self-contained systems with rules, citizens, currencies, and courts. They do what nations once claimed as exclusive rights: they mint their own money in the form of cryptocurrencies or tokenized assets; they regulate speech through moderation and algorithmic curation; they adjudicate disputes in closed systems of customer service and automated resolution; they extract tribute through subscriptions, fees, and behavioral data. Their laws are the Terms of Service. Their borders are user credentials. Their militaries are lines of code defending against intrusion.

To the modern Prince, clinging to the map of nation-states is an error of perspective. Power is no longer where it is printed, it is where it is *used*. The new cartography of control is drawn not in geography, but in *architecture*, the architecture of networks, of protocols, of attention. Where do people spend their time? Where do they transact? Where do they speak, shop, fall in love, learn, revolt, and confess? These are the coordinates of real power. And in this age, the people no longer live inside countries, they live inside platforms.

Sovereignty itself is being redefined. No longer is it measured by the ability to defend land or issue passports. Sovereignty now lies in *access*. To govern is to determine who may enter and who must be exiled. It is the power to grant or deny visibility, to amplify or suppress expression, to approve or suspend transactions. In every meaningful domain, commerce, communication, culture, the gatekeepers are not governments. They are platforms. And these platforms, for all their posturing as neutral tools, wield their power with all the authority of kings.

The implications are profound. A government can declare a law, but a platform can make it obsolete. A nation can assert its sovereignty, but if it cannot compel compliance from the systems its people depend on, if it cannot regulate the platforms that mediate every part of daily life, then it has already been outflanked. The locus of power has moved upstream, into the codebase. It has become ambient, automatic, and infrastructural. The interface has become the institution.

And unlike nations, platforms are not beholden to the rituals of democracy. They do not need to campaign, negotiate, or even explain.

They operate in opacity, scale without borders, and evolve faster than legislation can follow. Their sovereignty is not debated, it is accepted by default, consented to with a tap.

Thus, let the new ruler understand: to lead in this era, one must not think like a president, but like a product architect. The tools of dominion are no longer the instruments of statecraft, they are systems design, user flow, behavioral incentives, and uptime. The sovereign of the future is not the one who commands an army or raises a flag. It is the one who controls the platform the people cannot leave.

The Decline of the Nation-State

The erosion of the nation-state is not a sudden collapse, but a long, steady exhalation, a relinquishing of power that began decades ago and has accelerated with the rise of globalized networks. At one time, the state was the primary engine of authority: it raised armies, levied taxes, regulated markets, and defined the rights and obligations of its citizens. Its power, though imperfect, was absolute within its borders. But in an era defined by connectivity and code, that supremacy has been fragmented. The tools of governance have slipped into new hands, not seized by revolution, but rendered obsolete by innovation.

Traditional governments, shackled by geography, legacy systems, and slow-moving bureaucracies, now find themselves outmaneuvered by corporations that exist everywhere and nowhere, entities that operate not in regions, but in realms of infrastructure, logistics, data, and influence. These are not just companies; they are sovereign-like institutions that govern without governance, rule without election, and shape society without ever appearing on a ballot.

Consider Amazon. On the surface, it is a retailer. In practice, it is a vertically integrated state-in-disguise. It commands a sprawling logistics empire, a supply chain that stretches across continents, a labor force rivaling that of mid-sized nations, and a digital infrastructure so vital that even governments rent space in its cloud. AWS, Amazon Web Services, does not merely host websites; it powers hospitals, financial institutions, intelligence agencies, and national defense systems. When Amazon experiences downtime, critical state functions grind to a halt. No public referendum approved this dependency. No legislation defined it. And yet it is reality. Amazon answers not to voters or parliaments, but to shareholders and machine-learned efficiencies. Its decisions are guided less by public will than by predictive analytics and profit-maximizing algorithms. If it is not a government in name, it is one in function.

Facebook, now Meta, represents another kind of sovereignty, social and psychological. At its zenith, Facebook connected over 3 billion people, a population larger than any nation in history. It did not just facilitate communication; it curated it. It decided whose voice carried, whose post would be seen, which memories would resurface, and which narratives would be buried. Its influence is not symbolic, it is algorithmic. A simple adjustment to its engagement model has been linked to political upheaval, electoral swings, and outbreaks of violence. With no need for censorship in the traditional sense, Facebook governs attention, and through that, perception. What is seen becomes real. What is unseen ceases to exist. In many ways, it has become the Ministry of Truth for the digital world, except it is privately owned, centrally controlled, and bound by no civic charter.

Then there is Google, the epistemological power. When people seek to know, they do not turn to teachers, politicians, or priests. They turn to the search bar. Google is the first responder to every question, the curator of answers, the silent editor of collective memory. Its ranking algorithms shape human understanding at scale, often more profoundly than any national curriculum. What it elevates is learned; what it deprioritizes, forgotten. Its predictive models anticipate not only what we think, but what we will think. To control knowledge is to control possibility, and in this regard, Google holds sway over the future itself. No state university system, no national library, and no government education department can compete with its scope or its immediacy.

These platforms, Amazon, Meta, Google, and others, have achieved something once reserved for nation-builders and empire-forgers. They have created systems of governance outside the traditional political order. They mint currencies (literal and symbolic), define laws through terms of service, enforce norms through algorithmic behavior, and extract wealth through subscription and surveillance. They offer protection (in the form of security features), public utilities (in the form of services), and even citizenship (in the form of user identity). Most strikingly, they have established loyalty not through ideology or blood, but through functionality. The people do not rise in protest against them because the platforms serve them, efficiently, addictively, and without interruption.

This is what Machiavelli praised in the great Princes of history: the ability to create new institutions, to reorient the customs of a people, to substitute obedience with utility. The platform lords have done all of this, not with armies, but with interfaces. Not by storming palaces, but by building ecosystems. And they have done so without the permission of any traditional authority. There was no treaty that granted them dominion. No public vote. No coronation. Their sovereignty emerged not from consent, but from use. They became indispensable, and that, in the end, is the purest form of power.

The nation-state, in comparison, begins to resemble an artifact of a bygone era: reactive, territorial, slow. It clings to symbols of authority, borders, embassies, flags, while the real levers of influence have moved elsewhere. To the cloud. To the feed. To the platform.

When comparing the projected financial scales of Amazon, Alphabet (Google), and Meta (Facebook) to the Gross Domestic Product (GDP) of countries in 2025, we can approximate their standings based on available data. While direct comparisons have limitations due to differences between corporate revenues and national GDP calculations, such an analysis provides insight into the economic influence of these technology giants.

Amazon

Annual Revenue: In 2024, Amazon reported a net income of $59.2 billion, a 94.6% increase over the previous year. Assuming continued growth, Amazon's 2025 revenue could be substantial, potentially approaching the GDP of countries like Norway or Austria, which have projected GDPs in the range of $500 to $600 billion.
-24/7 Wall St.

Alphabet (Google)

Annual Revenue: Analysts project that Google's search advertising revenue will grow nearly 10% to $216.5 billion in 2025. This figure suggests that Alphabet's total revenue could rival the GDP of countries such as Finland or Portugal, whose economies are projected to be in the vicinity of $200 to $250 billion.
-Investor's Business Daily

Meta (Facebook)

Annual Revenue: Meta's revenue growth is expected to slow, with analysts projecting a 14.5% increase in 2025, compared to a 23.4% jump in the previous year. If Meta's 2024 revenue was approximately $117 billion, a 14.5% increase would result in around $134 billion for 2025. This would place Meta's revenue on par with the GDP of countries like Hungary or Ukraine, which have economies projected in the $130 to $150 billion range.
-Investor's Business Daily

These comparisons underscore the immense economic scale of leading technology companies, highlighting that their annual revenues can rival or surpass the economic outputs of entire nations.

Platforms as Sovereign Entities

The modern platform is not merely a tool of communication or commerce; it is, in the truest sense, a sovereign entity. It does not simply facilitate activity, it governs it. In structure, in scope, and in function, the platform mirrors the classical elements of statehood. It possesses territory, not in the form of land, but through digital real estate, cloud infrastructure, and the very architecture of its interface. Where users go, what they see, and how they interact is dictated entirely by the design choices of the platform, creating a controlled environment more akin to a walled city than an open commons.

Its population consists of subjects, users, creators, followers, and sellers, who participate in its economy, abide by its rules, and are shaped by its incentives. These are not passive audiences; they are active citizens of a digital realm, bound to a platform's rhythms and rituals. The platform sets the law through terms of service, moderation protocols, and community guidelines. These edicts are binding, often more so than national laws, because they operate continuously and ubiquitously. The rules may change at any time, and yet all are expected to comply instantly.

Platforms also mint their own currencies, often in forms that blend finance and influence, advertising credits, digital tokens, NFTs, subscription points, and micropayment systems. These currencies circulate within the ecosystem, creating internal economies that resemble feudal tax systems. Just as medieval lords demanded tribute in grain or coin, platforms extract value in clicks, content, and cash. And where there is law, there is enforcement. Platforms do not rely on courts or police; they wield automated justice through shadowbans, AI surveillance, and algorithmic punishment. A user can be exiled from a platform in an instant, without appeal, silenced not by judge or jury, but by code.

Borders exist as well, though they are not marked by fences. They are shaped by onboarding flows, account verification, regional restrictions, and proprietary ecosystems. Crossing into a platform requires consent, identity, and sometimes loyalty. Diplomacy, too, is alive in the platform age. Instead of embassies and treaties, we find API agreements, cross-platform integrations, strategic mergers, and licensing deals, alliances formed not between nations, but between systems. And finally, there is tribute: platforms demand payment not just in currency, but in attention, time, and data. Subscriptions, transaction fees, user analytics, all are forms of tribute paid by subjects to their digital sovereigns.

A modern Prince must grasp this reality. The platform is the new organized society. Where once a castle housed the power of a baron, the platform now hosts entire economies, cultural movements, behavioral norms, and hierarchies of influence. These new realms may coexist with the state, but only uneasily. In many cases, they outpace and overshadow it, quietly absorbing its relevance.

The citizen of yesterday voted every four years; the digital subject of today interacts with platforms every hour. His speech is filtered, his preferences nudged, his transactions taxed, not by a public government, but by private algorithms. He lives under the rule of unseen lords, their edicts embedded in code. And where the state operates with sluggish transparency, the platform moves with silent speed. A law may take months to debate and pass. A platform can alter its rules overnight, with no deliberation, no consent, just a notification, a check box, an "Agree" button. And with that, a new law is passed.

This is not dystopia. It is not fiction. It is the present. The platform is no longer a tool, it is the throne.

Identity and Allegiance in a Platform World

We must now confront a question once considered unthinkable in political philosophy: to whom are the people truly loyal? In earlier centuries, the answer was simple, loyalty belonged to the crown, the republic, the homeland. Allegiance was tethered to geography, tradition, and shared myth. But in the digital age, that clarity has dissolved. Identity, once rooted in soil and flag, now floats freely in the cloud.

Consider this: if an individual spends more waking hours on Discord servers than in their local community, if their primary income comes not from a factory or office, but from YouTube monetization or Substack subscriptions, if their worldview, sense of humor, aesthetic tastes, and moral compass are all shaped by TikTok's algorithmic feed, what exactly binds them to the nation-state? What role does the state still play in their daily experience, their emotional life, their future planning?

Nationality has become an aesthetic, not an organizing principle. It is visible at the Olympics, on a passport, during patriotic holidays, but it is increasingly irrelevant in the actual flow of life. Platforms, by contrast, do not merely host activity, they mediate reality itself. They curate emotion, filter memory, organize social connections, and define what is visible or invisible in the cultural landscape. They are not tools of communication. They are the environments in which modern existence unfolds.

Just as medieval peasants knew the name of their local lord more intimately than that of their distant monarch, so too does the modern subject today know the quirks of Instagram's engagement algorithm better than the articles of their constitution. They are more concerned about whether their post will be shadowbanned than whether their privacy rights have been abridged by legislation. A change to TikTok's trend mechanics provokes more reaction than a change in tax policy. The authority that governs emotion, income, identity, and even social cohesion no longer resides in a national capital, it resides in the cloud, distributed across platforms, protocols, and private code.

This shift is not symbolic. It is structural. It marks the transformation of allegiance from state to system, from citizen to user. The nation-state is no longer the primary mediator of reality; it is one voice among many, and increasingly, it is the quietest in the room.

The modern Prince must understand this above all. You cannot claim to rule if you do not understand where your people live. And today, they live not in the nation, but in the network. The bonds of patriotism have weakened. The bonds of interface have strengthened. Culture is shaped in feeds, not in town halls. Power is expressed through UX updates, not executive orders.

So, if you would govern, if you would hold influence in this new epoch, do not ask where your people were born. Do not ask what anthem they sing. Ask where they log in. Because that is where their loyalty now lies.

As of 2025, Americans' engagement with online entertainment platforms varies notably across different age groups, reflecting distinct media consumption habits.

General Population

On average, U.S. consumers dedicate approximately six hours daily to media and entertainment. This encompasses activities such as streaming videos, engaging with social media, gaming, and listening to music or podcasts.

-Deloitte United States

Generation Z (Ages 9-24)

Generation Z stands out for its substantial media consumption, averaging about 6.6 hours per day. Notably, some individuals within this group report engaging with content for up to 15 hours daily.
-New York Post

Teenagers

Teenagers from lower-income households (annual income under $35,000) exhibit higher screen time, averaging 9 hours and 19 minutes daily. In contrast, their peers from higher-income families (annual income over $100,000) average 7 hours and 16 minutes per day.

-Exploding Topics

Young Adults (Ages 18-24)

Young adults in the 18-24 age range spend an average of 22 minutes daily on Facebook. This demographic shows a preference for platforms like TikTok and Snapchat for their daily social interactions.
-Sprout Social

Children (Ages 0-8)

For younger children, the average daily screen time remains around 2.5 hours. However, there's a noticeable shift from traditional television viewing to activities such as gaming and watching short-form videos on platforms like TikTok and Instagram Reels.
-Parents

These insights underscore the evolving landscape of media consumption in the U.S., highlighting the increasing influence of digital platforms across various age groups.

Determining the exact amount of time the average American dedicates to learning about the U.S. Constitution and the functions of government over their lifetime is challenging due to limited comprehensive data. However, by examining available information on educational requirements and general civic knowledge, we can make informed estimates.

Formal Education

Civics education varies significantly across the United States. Only nine states and the District of Columbia mandate a full year of U.S. government or civics education. The majority, 31 states, require only a half-year, and 10 states have no specific civics requirement.
-Annenberg Public Policy Center and Center for American Progress

Assuming a half-year course entails approximately one hour of instruction per school day over a semester (roughly 90 days), students receive about 90 hours of formal civics education during their schooling.

In states with a full-year requirement, this would double to approximately 180 hours.

Civic Knowledge and Engagement

Despite these educational efforts, surveys reveal gaps in civic knowledge among Americans. For instance, a 2023 Annenberg Public Policy Center survey found that only 66% of U.S. adults could name all three branches of government, and just 77% could identify freedom of speech as a right guaranteed by the First Amendment.

-Pew Research Center, Annenberg Public Policy Center, and Big Think

While precise lifetime totals are elusive, formal education hours suggests that the average American spends a limited amount of time, potentially a few hundred hours over their lifetime, focused specifically on understanding the U.S. Constitution and government functions.

V

Code is Law

The Eclipse of Traditional Law. In the age of techno-feudalism, power no longer emanates from traditional seats of authority alone. It does not flow strictly from thrones or elected chambers, nor from constitutions or charters. Instead, it radiates, often invisibly, from the lines of code that govern our digital environments. Once, it was the signature of a monarch or the passing of a statute that determined what could or could not be done. Today, that role has been largely assumed by software, algorithms, and platform protocols that enforce behavior automatically and relentlessly. The old legal systems still exist, but they are increasingly ceremonial, overshadowed by a new kind of rule, one that executes instantly, without trial, and without human discretion. It is law at the speed of light, enforced by machines without pause or pity.

This transformation did not arrive with fanfare. It crept in quietly, embedded in apps, interfaces, and backend systems. It was predicted decades ago by early thinkers of the digital age who understood that the absence of government regulation online did not imply the absence of regulation itself. On the contrary: the vacuum left by governments was swiftly filled by code. As one digital legal theorist famously observed, "Code is law." That is, the very structure of software dictates what can and cannot be done online, what actions are allowed, what speech is visible, and what identities are valid. And unlike legal systems shaped by centuries of philosophical debate, democratic participation, or public accountability, the rules of code are written by engineers and product managers behind closed doors.

— CODE IS LAW

The modern Prince must recognize this tectonic shift. Where kings once used armies and judges to impose their will, platforms now use scripts and APIs. Their power is not asserted through physical force but through architecture, architectures of access, engagement, and enforcement. The new edicts are not posted in courthouses; they are embedded in platforms' Terms of Service, often unread yet universally binding. These digital decrees are not debated in public forums, they are quietly updated, instantly adopted, and enforced without warning. The result is a form of governance that is more pervasive than the state, and in many ways, more efficient.

What makes this power uniquely formidable is the nature of code itself. Code does not deliberate. It does not show leniency. It does not consider context, motive, or extenuating circumstance. It does not offer mercy. Traditional law allows for human interpretation, a judge may weigh a case, a jury may dissent, an appeal may offer recourse. But code acts blindly. It is binary. If a condition is met, a consequence follows. If a post triggers a moderation rule, it is deleted. If a user violates an opaque policy, their access is revoked. There is no courtroom, no counsel, no closing statement, only execution.

This mechanized form of judgment reshapes the relationship between ruler and subject. In the techno-feudal order, power is not simply held, it is embedded. The interface becomes the courtroom. The algorithm becomes the magistrate. And the user becomes both citizen and data point, governed by rules they neither understand nor negotiate. A single line of code, deployed across a platform's infrastructure, can impact millions, altering what is seen, what is silenced, what is sold. A well-placed "if-then" condition in the system may carry more weight than a hundred laws passed through a legislature.

We are witnessing not the disappearance of law, but its privatization. Just as medieval lords enforced justice on their estates through personal codes and arbitrary penalties, so too do modern platforms enforce private law across their digital territories. Facebook, YouTube, TikTok, these are not mere services. They are self-contained polities with their own constitutions, courts, currencies, and police forces. Their users live under their jurisdiction not metaphorically, but materially. And unlike states, which are theoretically accountable to their citizens, platforms answer only to shareholders, engagement metrics, or internal policies.

Nowhere is this more vividly illustrated than in the unprecedented banishment of a sitting head of state from a platform. In early 2021, the President of the United States, arguably the most powerful man in the world, was removed from major social media platforms. No government tribunal delivered the judgment. No legislative body held a vote. It was a unilateral act of corporate enforcement, carried out by a private company executing its own rules. The implications were profound: the sovereign of a nation had been subordinated to the sovereign of a platform. As legal scholars quickly pointed out, the First Amendment does not apply to private companies. These platforms, legally, were free to silence whomever they chose. And so they did.

This is the essence of techno-feudal law. The platform's rules override the nation's in practice, if not in theory. A digital lord can exile anyone, from the anonymous troll to the elected president, with no trial, no warning, no appeal. These are not just isolated acts of moderation. They are political events. And they make clear that in the digital realm, sovereignty resides with those who control the infrastructure, not those who hold office.

For the modern Prince, this reality demands a new kind of literacy. Mastery of the political now requires fluency in the technical. To govern effectively, one must understand not only human nature, but the logic of algorithms and the architecture of platforms. Influence is no longer secured solely through charisma, rhetoric, or ideology. It is secured through control of systems, through the placement of rules within code, the design of interfaces, and the management of data flows. In this environment, a savvy ruler need not command a standing army. He needs only command a development team.

This chapter, then, is not merely about code as law. It is about law as code, and about what it means to lead when governance is automated, when justice is outsourced to machines, and when citizenship itself is mediated by private platforms. In this world, the most powerful are not those who legislate, but those who program. And the most successful rulers will be those who learn to write in code, or, at the very least, those who understand how to rule through those who do.

IV. The Power to Exile

One of the oldest and most profound expressions of sovereignty has always been the power to exile. In the traditional order of kings and courts, exile was more than punishment, it was obliteration from the social fabric. To be banished was to lose not just one's rights, but one's place in the world. You could no longer speak in the public square, no longer trade in the market, no longer live among others as a recognized member of society. Exile was the erasure of a person's presence from the collective life of a community. It required the authority of a sovereign, the formality of legal judgment, and the force of law.

Today, exile has been redefined. It is no longer handed down by monarchs or magistrates, nor does it necessarily involve borders or physical displacement. In the digital age, exile is platform-based. And though it may not involve the loss of physical territory, it often results in something even more devastating, the erasure of digital identity, income, and influence.

To be banned from what was once called Twitter (now X) is not merely to lose access to a website; it is to be cut off from public discourse. It is the modern equivalent of being silenced in the town square. For many, their voice, audience, and ability to influence others' lives on these platforms. Removal means invisibility.

To be deplatformed from YouTube goes beyond losing a channel, it can mean the loss of one's livelihood. For countless creators, YouTube is not just a place to express ideas, it is their primary source of income, a business model, and an ecosystem of fans, advertisers, and collaborators. Removal is economic decapitation.

To be banned from Amazon as a seller is to be exiled from the largest marketplace in the modern world. It is not just the loss of a storefront, it is the loss of access to a global consumer base, logistics infrastructure, and the engine of modern commerce. In this context, a ban is akin to being barred from operating a business at all.

To be removed from PayPal, or any dominant digital payment processor, is to lose the ability to transact. It is to be economically paralyzed. If you cannot send or receive funds, you are effectively cast out of the economy, unable to participate in even the most basic functions of modern life. It is financial exile.

To be de-indexed or removed from Google is perhaps the most profound form of digital invisibility. It is not simply the suppression of a page, but the erasure of presence. If you cannot be found, you do not exist in the digital realm. Whether you are a business, a public figure, or an activist, exclusion from search is a form of digital unpersoning.

What's most critical for the modern Prince to understand is that this form of exile does not follow the old rituals of law and punishment. There is no formal charge, no hearing, no trial. Exile today is enacted through automated systems, algorithmic moderation, or trust-and-safety teams operating behind closed doors. The decision may be justified by vague policy violations, but there is often no meaningful recourse, no jury, no appeals process, no accountability. A person can wake up to find their accounts terminated and their access revoked, without warning or explanation.

This new form of exile is often more totalizing than its historical counterpart. A citizen who is imprisoned by the state retains legal status. They can appeal, write letters, vote, receive visitors. They remain, in some way, within the moral and legal imagination of society. But a user banned by a platform is rendered functionally nonexistent. Their income may vanish, their network may collapse, and their digital history may be erased. They become a ghost in the machine, no longer able to speak, sell, or interact within the dominant channels of modern life.

This shift represents a seismic transformation in how power is enacted and experienced. It reveals that platforms, not states, now wield the most immediate and intimate forms of control. And for the ruler who aspires to power in this digital age, this lesson is critical: a sovereign who does not control the mechanisms of digital exile is a sovereign only in name. Authority today is not expressed through thrones or flags, but through admin dashboards and moderation queues. To rule effectively, one must be able to silence, suspend, or ban, to exile, not with armies, but with interfaces.

In the end, exile is no longer a political act rendered visible by spectacle. It is a technical function, executed with a click. And its consequences are no less profound for their silence.

Platform as Infrastructure

The true power of platforms lies not in likes, followers, or the surface-level engagement metrics of user activity, but in the deep and often invisible infrastructure they now control. These companies have evolved far beyond their origins as consumer-facing brands or digital storefronts. They are no longer simply purveyors of content or gadgets; they are the architects and gatekeepers of the systems upon which modern civilization now runs. Increasingly, the core functions that were once the domain of states, transportation, communication, finance, logistics, security, have been quietly outsourced to private technology firms. These firms do not just shape the digital landscape. They constitute its foundation.

Amazon, through its cloud computing division, Amazon Web Services (AWS), has become the nervous system of the internet. It powers not only the fledgling dreams of startups, but the bureaucratic and operational machinery of governments, militaries, and global institutions. Defense departments, intelligence agencies, and public health systems all rely on AWS servers to process data, run applications, and maintain operational continuity. If AWS were to go dark or be withdrawn from any one of these entities, the result would not be a mere inconvenience, it would be a national emergency. In some cases, it could rival the disruption of a hostile cyberattack.

Google Maps, too, is no longer just a tool for finding coffee shops or avoiding traffic. It has become the invisible spine of global logistics. Commercial fleets, emergency services, drone navigation systems, rideshare networks, and even military operations rely on its mapping infrastructure. When a truck is dispatched, when a missile is guided, when a consumer chooses a restaurant, it is often Google Maps that determines the route, the timing, and even the destination. To alter or restrict access to this platform would mean not just interfering with convenience, it would be to redirect the movement of people, goods, and weapons.

Financial power has also shifted. Apple Pay and Stripe now serve as intermediaries in billions of transactions, handling the movement of capital across borders and ecosystems. These platforms are not just digital wallets, they are financial gateways, deciding who gets to pay, who gets paid, and under what conditions. Their protocols are private, their policies unaccountable, and yet they underpin the flow of global commerce with a reach that surpasses many traditional banks or regulatory institutions.

Then there are entities like Cloudflare and Akamai, companies most people have never heard of, yet whose decisions dictate whether a website remains online or vanishes. These firms provide critical web infrastructure services such as content delivery, load balancing, and protection from cyberattacks. If they withdraw support from a client, that client's entire digital presence can collapse instantly. Their power is not visible on a homepage, it lives in the code, in the packets, in the speed and survivability of websites themselves. They do not merely protect the internet, they decide, in effect, who gets to exist on it.

Meta, formerly Facebook, is not just a social network, it has become a system of identity verification, a tool for civic mobilization, and the default advertising infrastructure for political and commercial campaigns alike. For billions of people, Meta is the platform through which they present themselves to the world, access social services, promote their businesses, and even authenticate who they are. This gives the company immense leverage, not only over individuals, but over entire populations. If it shifts its policies or tweaks its algorithms, entire communities can be elevated or erased from the public eye.

What emerges from this landscape is a stark truth: the fundamental operations of contemporary life, those once guarded by public institutions, are now managed by private corporations. These companies do not merely offer products or services. They own the pipes and protocols. They set the standards. They hold the keys.

And unlike states, they are not answerable to the citizenry. Their decisions are made in boardrooms, not parliaments. Their executives are beholden to shareholders, not voters. They can enforce bans, deny access, or modify critical functions without oversight, transparency, or appeal. If Amazon were to terminate cloud services for a nation's government infrastructure, the consequences would echo those of a strategic cyberwarfare strike. If Google were to alter its search algorithm to deprioritize dissenting viewpoints, it could reshape public discourse itself, without needing to change a single law.

The Prince must see this landscape with clarity. Sovereignty in this age does not only reside in territorial control, in flags or legislative bodies. It resides in infrastructure. Control the data centers, the APIs, the payment gateways, the verification protocols, and you control the realm. Modern power is no longer maintained by controlling borders, but by controlling the platforms that define where people work, speak, trade, and live.

To rule effectively in this world, one must understand that power flows not only through charisma or conquest, but through backend systems and platform dependencies. To lose access to infrastructure is to lose the ability to function in modern life. Thus, for the digital ruler, technical control is political control. And to govern in the 21st century is to govern through systems.

The Church and the State: A Historic Parallel

To understand the peculiar shape of power in our current era, we must look backward, not to the Enlightenment or the Industrial Revolution, but deeper into the Middle Ages. For it is there, in the feudal world of kings and cathedrals, that we find a structure that closely resembles our own. In that age, authority was divided between two realms: the secular and the spiritual. Kings and emperors ruled over physical territories, collected taxes, raised armies, and enforced laws. But the Catholic Church ruled something more elusive and arguably more enduring, it ruled the soul.

The Church was not a mere religious institution. It was a parallel system of governance that transcended borders and outlasted dynasties. It had its own legal framework, known as canon law, which often superseded or conflicted with local laws. It operated its own courts, independent of royal justice. It levied its own taxes, tithes extracted from the faithful under threat of spiritual consequence. It even had its own currency of sorts: indulgences, spiritual credits that could be purchased to reduce punishment in the afterlife. In some cases, indulgences were traded like bonds, spiritual assets with political implications.

The Church maintained its own army. The Crusaders were not only religious warriors but also instruments of geopolitical power, marching under the banner of divine will. It had its own official language, Latin, which unified the literate elite across kingdoms, and ensured that interpretation of texts, rituals, and doctrine remained centralized and controlled. Most importantly, the Church held a monopoly on meaning. It alone interpreted the sacred texts, defined the moral order, and claimed exclusive authority over salvation.

A king might command armies, but if he crossed the Church, he risked excommunication, a form of existential exile. To be excommunicated was not just to be banned from religious rites; it was to be made illegitimate in the eyes of one's people. The king could not be married, could not be buried on sacred ground, and in many cases, could not rule. Trade could be halted, alliances broken, revolts inspired. Excommunication was the medieval equivalent of deplatforming, and it carried the same devastating weight: to be cast out of the structure that granted legitimacy, visibility, and belonging.

This medieval dual-power structure, a secular system of force and a spiritual system of meaning, finds its modern echo in the relationship between nation-states and digital platforms. Today's platforms are not merely economic players or technological tools. They are systems of symbolic and social authority. Governments may still hold sway over borders and budgets, but platforms control attention, perception, identity, and belief. They mediate what is seen, what is shared, what is silenced, and what is remembered.

Platforms now operate with many of the same features once reserved for the medieval Church. They possess their own laws, written in Terms of Service and enforced without appeal. They run their own courts, from moderation queues to automated content rulings. They levy their own taxes, whether through data extraction, transaction fees, or ad monetization. They possess their own languages, code, UI, algorithmic logic, that only the initiated truly understand. And they traffic in their own currency not indulgences, but metrics, followers, likes, views, impressions, trust scores. These are the digital equivalents of spiritual merit, determining one's status, reach, and perceived worth in the online world.

Just as the Church of old did not merely enforce moral rules, but defined the very categories of sin and virtue, platforms now define what counts as "misinformation," "harmful content," or "trusted sources." They do not just react to culture, they shape it. They do not simply moderate speech; they dictate the parameters of permissible thought. They issue algorithmic indulgences to those who align with their norms and shadowban the heretics who do not. They hold the power to declare someone socially dead without explanation or process.

This is why the modern ruler must study not only the kings and emperors of history, but also the popes. For in this new order, Mark

Zuckerberg, Sundar Pichai, Elon Musk, and others are not merely CEOs, they are High Priests of the Protocol. Their role is closer to that of Pope Gregory VII than that of a traditional executive. They preside over vast digital congregations, define moral orthodoxy, and enforce obedience through ritual, design, and code.

In such a world, political power alone is insufficient. The modern Prince must grasp the logic of platform authority, understand how legitimacy is manufactured algorithmically, and recognize that sovereignty now operates in two planes: the material and the digital, the legal and the symbolic, the territorial and the emotional. The state may command force, but the platform commands faith. And in a world where most people live partially or even primarily online, it is faith, perception, meaning, and narrative, that ultimately governs action.

Thus, the Prince who would rule today must do more than govern territory. He must learn to govern attention. He must not only master law, but doctrine. For to ignore the spiritual dimension of platform power is to misunderstand the very architecture of modern control.

And that architecture, like the medieval Church, is not built on consensus. It is built on authority cloaked in benevolence, enforced through ritual, and sustained by faith. Faith not in God, but in the interface.

How Platforms Supersede Governments

To understand the transformation of power in the digital age, we must confront a startling reality: in many crucial domains, platforms have not only rivaled but surpassed the traditional powers of government. While states still claim the authority of law, borders, and flags, it is increasingly the platforms that dictate the rhythms of daily life, the flow of information, and the architecture of opportunity. This is not a symbolic shift, it is a structural one. Let us consider, in detail, how platforms have outpaced the institutions that once defined civilization.

First, there is the matter of speed. A government bound by legislative procedure must move slowly by design. Laws require drafting, debate, negotiation, passage, implementation, a process that may take months or even years. A platform, by contrast, can alter its policies overnight. A single decision made in a boardroom or by an executive team can redefine the rules of engagement for billions of people with no vote, no hearing, and no notice. A single software patch or policy update, deployed quietly in the night, can have a more immediate impact than an entire year of government reform. In this context, platforms are not just faster, they are temporally dominant.

Next, consider scale. The reach of a government is limited by jurisdiction. A president's speech is filtered through press conferences, media outlets, and national boundaries. But a tweet from a tech CEO, unmediated, algorithmically amplified, can travel faster and further, shaping public perception globally within minutes. The audience is not just a constituency, it is the world. In a matter of seconds, the words of a platform executive can move markets, provoke outrage, or launch cultural trends. Scale once belonged to empires. Now it belongs to feeds.

Then there is the matter of data. No intelligence agency or census bureau in history has collected as much information about human behavior as today's platforms. Every click, swipe, search, and share is recorded, parsed, and analyzed. These platforms know not just what people do, but what they want, what they fear, what they are likely to do next. They hold detailed psychological profiles of billions of users, and data more intimate and predictive than anything a government has ever possessed. This knowledge is power, and it is entirely in private hands.

Monetary control has also begun to shift. Central banks were once the undisputed stewards of currency and economic stability. But the rise of fintech and decentralized technologies has enabled platforms to mint, manage, and move money outside of traditional financial systems. From mobile payment platforms to cryptocurrencies to in-app tipping systems, the mechanics of economic exchange are now deeply embedded in private infrastructure. Entire economies operate within platform ecosystems, where transactions are governed not by law, but by Terms of Service.

Justice, too, has been redefined. The state traditionally enforces law through a visible system of courts, trials, and due process. But on platforms, justice is automated. An AI detects a violation, renders a judgment, and delivers a penalty, all within milliseconds. There is no judge, no defense, no appeal. You are banned, demonetized, or silenced before you even know what happened. The architecture of enforcement has become invisible, instant, and absolute. It is justice without law, punishment without trial.

Control of the media has likewise shifted. Platforms are no longer just conduits for news, they are its architects. Algorithms determine what stories are promoted, which narratives are buried, and whose voices are heard. The feed has become the front page, the editorial board, and the censor. Traditional media outlets, once arbiters of public discourse, now beg for visibility inside algorithmic ecosystems they do not control. Reality is not what is true, it is what the platform delivers.

Even national security, once the sovereign realm of the state, now depends on platform infrastructure. Modern warfare requires cloud computing, global communication, cybersecurity, satellite mapping, and data storage, all of which are increasingly outsourced to private tech companies.

The Pentagon runs on Amazon Web Services.

Amazon Web Services (AWS) has solidified its position as a cornerstone of Amazon's business operations, demonstrating substantial growth in recent years. In 2024, AWS achieved net sales of $107.6 billion, marking a 19% increase from the previous year's $90.8 billion. This upward trajectory continued into the fourth quarter of 2024, with AWS reporting sales of $28.8 billion, up from $24.2 billion in the same quarter of 2023.

-Data Center Dynamics

The profitability of AWS is equally noteworthy. In 2024, the segment's operating income reached $39.8 billion, a significant rise from $24.6 billion in 2023. During the fourth quarter of 2024 alone, AWS's operating income was $10.6 billion, compared to $7.2 billion in the corresponding quarter of the previous year.
-Data Center Dynamics and Amazon Investor Relations

These figures underscore AWS's critical role within Amazon's overall financial performance. As of 2023, AWS accounted for approximately 15.8% of Amazon's total net sales. Given its consistent growth, AWS's contribution to Amazon's revenue and profitability is expected to remain substantial.

Intelligence operations rely on Google infrastructure.

Google has recently achieved significant milestones in providing cloud services to U.S. defense and intelligence agencies. In April 2024, Google Public Sector announced that its air-gapped cloud platform, Google Distributed Cloud Hosted (GDC Hosted), received authorization to handle top-secret workloads for the Department of Defense (DoD) and both secret and top-secret missions for intelligence agencies.
-LinkedIn, Nextgov/FCW, FedScoop, Intelligence Community News

GDC Hosted is designed to meet the stringent security requirements of U.S. government customers, offering integrated cloud services such as compute, storage, and advanced AI tools. This platform enables agencies to process sensitive data securely while leveraging Google's technological capabilities.
-Intelligence Community News, LinkedIn, and FedScoop

Furthermore, in December 2022, the DoD awarded the Joint Warfighting Cloud Capability (JWCC) contract to multiple vendors, including Google, Amazon, Microsoft, and Oracle. This $9 billion contract aims to provide the DoD with a multi-vendor, multi-cloud environment to support various defense operations.

While these developments highlight Google's expanding role in supporting U.S. intelligence and defense operations, specific details regarding the scale and scope of Google's infrastructure dedicated to these activities remain classified and are not publicly disclosed. This confidentiality is standard practice to maintain operational security within intelligence operations. The state may still deploy troops, but without the platforms, it cannot see, coordinate, or respond. The battlefield has moved into the server room.

Finally, the realm of employment, perhaps the most tangible function of state and economy alike, has been fundamentally transformed. People no longer work for companies in the traditional sense. Increasingly, they work on platforms. Etsy, Uber, TikTok, Substack, these are not just marketplaces. They are employers, regulators, and tax collectors rolled into one. They define the rules of engagement, the pay structure, and the path to visibility. They issue rewards and penalties, shape professional identities, and control access to opportunity. For many, the platform is both their boss and their bureaucrat.

What emerges from this constellation of powers is a new anatomy of governance. If the state is the body politic, then the platform is its nervous system, carrying signals, enforcing responses, directing behavior. And crucially, this nervous system is no longer fully connected to the head. It operates independently, without the traditional checks and balances of democratic governance. It is responsive not to voters or laws, but to internal metrics, shareholder interests, and machine-optimized outcomes.

In this light, the modern Prince must revise their concept of sovereignty. To control territory is no longer enough. One must control the systems of immediacy, the architecture of perception, and the invisible flows of capital, data, and meaning. Power today resides not just in the palace or the parliament, but in the platform. And the one who commands the platform commands the world.

Strategic Advice to the Modern Prince

A ruler who wishes to endure, let alone dominate, in the age of platforms must abandon both illusion and nostalgia. The idealist, who believes the internet is a neutral commons or a bastion of free expression, will be crushed by systems that reward conformity, not conviction. The Luddite, who rejects technology in favor of tradition, will soon find that tradition has been unmoored from relevance. The sovereign of this era must see clearly: platforms are not extensions of the world. They are the world, and to rule today is to rule within, through, and sometimes against them.

To govern in this new domain requires more than policy, it requires strategy, adaptability, and a cold understanding of where power now resides. And so, here is your counsel, drawn not from sentiment, but from necessity.

The first principle is this: secure platform alliances. Just as kings of old formed treaties with neighboring monarchs to preserve peace and gain influence, so too must the modern ruler cultivate relationships with those who control the platforms. These are not CEOs in the traditional sense; they are digital aristocrats, high priests of protocol, whose decisions reverberate globally within seconds. Treat them not as merchants but as peers in power. Approach them with strategic respect. Flatter their innovations, offer shared interests, entangle their prosperity with your own. If you rise together, you rise safely. But if you provoke them without leverage, they will silence you with a switch. Better a quiet accord than a loud defeat.

Yet no ruler survives solely on the favor of others. Alliances are useful, but autonomy is essential. When possible, build your own platform, your own domain of influence, where your laws are final, and your infrastructure is sovereign. A ruler who depends on the tools of others, who builds his power on YouTube channels or Shopify storefronts, is no king, he is a tenant farmer, working someone else's land. Do not mistake visibility for ownership. If your castle stands on another's server, it can be razed at any moment. Build your own stack. Own your list, your content, your pipeline. Rule not as a guest, but as a lord.

To govern a digital domain is to manage its borders. Power lies in the ability to decide who belongs and who does not. So, control entry and exit. Gatekeeping is not cruelty, it is cultivation. Onboarding should be deliberate, not indiscriminate. Every member of your realm changes its culture. Be selective. Similarly, exile should be strategic, not reactive. Remove those who threaten the order, who sabotage cohesion, who dilute the mission. Platforms thrive because they determine who enters and who is removed. You must do the same. The sovereign defines the citizenry.

If you wish to operate within the great platforms of today, you must learn their true legal systems: the Terms of Service. These are not incidental documents, they are constitutions, often more binding than national law. Read them not as consumers do, but as tacticians. Study them like scripture. Interpret their ambiguities. Within every clause lies a loophole, a lever, a landmine. Understand them better than their enforcers do. Use their rules against them when necessary. Obey when it serves you; subvert when it does not. Every system has cracks. The wise ruler finds them before his rivals do.

But knowledge of law is nothing without visibility. In the age of platforms, to be invisible is to be irrelevant. A buried message is as powerless as a silenced one. You must learn how visibility is engineered, how algorithms determine what rises and what vanishes. Study the mechanics of attention: how search is optimized, how engagement is rewarded, how velocity creates authority. Learn the language of metrics. Or, if you cannot, align yourself with those who can. Influence today is not declared; it is surfaced. To rule is to be seen.

Even the most careful sovereign can be exiled, so prepare for the inevitable. Protect against deplatforming not as a possibility, but as a certainty. Build redundancies. Diversify your reach. Maintain email lists. Mirror your content. Own your domains. Invest in analog relationships and offline influence. Be ready to vanish from one space and reappear in another. A wise ruler prepares for digital exile as a wartime prince prepares for siege, not with panic, but with planning.

The future does not yet belong to the giants. It belongs to those who move first. Colonize new platforms early. Enter emerging territories, AI worlds, blockchain protocols, immersive virtual realms, before they are governed. The first to arrive does not follow the rules; he writes them. Stake your claim before the map is drawn. Establish the language, the norms, the power structures. Become the native authority, so that others arrive as guests in your domain. To shape the future, you must plant flags in unclaimed soil.

And finally, understand this truth: platforms are not utilities. They are not neutral infrastructures or impartial tools. They are sovereign entities. They are states in everything but name. Treat them as such. Negotiate with them as powers. Pressure them when necessary. Subsidize them when useful. Co-opt their protocols or build alternatives to them. Just as the ruler of a nation must navigate international diplomacy, so too must the ruler of a digital domain engage with the empires of code that now define reality.

This is the age of platforms. It is an age of soft empires, invisible borders, and algorithmic law. To rule in this age is not to raise an army or win an election. It is to master systems, command narratives, control flows of data and meaning.

The path forward is not for the nostalgic. It is for the sovereign who understands that thrones now live in dashboards, that kingdoms are shaped by protocols, and that the seat of power has shifted, not into the hands of governments, but into the hands of those who control the feed.

You must not merely survive this world. You must learn to rule it.

The Network Crown

In centuries past, the path to power was clearly marked. A man who wished to rule needed the symbols and tools of authority: a sword to enforce his will, a title to legitimize his claim, or a rebellion to upend the existing order. Thrones were seized by force or inheritance, and dominion was measured in acres, armies, and allegiances. The world was ruled by those who could lay claim to territory, command loyalty, and, when needed, crush opposition.

But today, the path is quieter, faster, and less visible. Power no longer rides on horseback or marches in ranks, it logs in. The modern prince does not storm a palace; he accesses a dashboard. He does not overthrow kings; he adjusts policies, modifies algorithms, and updates user permissions. A single change in the back end of a major platform, a tweak to visibility, a shift in verification, an alteration in onboarding, can have more impact on a population than a thousand-page bill passed through parliament. In this world, to wield power is not to hold a sword, but to hold the keys.

The prince of the present, and of the future, must stop asking how to govern the nation. That question belongs to a fading world. He must instead ask: Which platform already governs the nation? Because the levers of governance have migrated. They are no longer housed solely in state capitals or national assemblies. They reside in the backend infrastructure of apps and services, in the quiet decisions made by engineers, product managers, and AI models. The power to shape behavior, direct flows of information, and define legitimacy has been ceded to platforms, quietly, efficiently, and, for the most part, willingly.

To understand this shift, one must look beyond the surface. Who owns the communication layer? That is, who decides what speech is amplified or silenced? Is it the elected official giving a press conference, or the platform deciding whether that video appears in your feed? Who owns the payment rails? Who controls the infrastructure that enables commerce, the flow of money, subscriptions, donations, wages? If a person cannot be paid, they cannot participate. And who owns the authentication layer? Who determines who is real, who is allowed in, who is verified, and who is banned? These are not abstract technical concerns. These are the foundations of sovereignty.

For whoever controls these layers governs the people, not in theory, but in practice. Governance today is not declared with constitutions but embedded in code. It is not enforced by law, but by protocols. The user agreement has replaced the royal decree. The update log is the new edict. The "Terms of Service" is a binding law, accepted daily, automatically, without reading, without debate. And those who control the platform control those terms.

The map of power, once drawn in blood and ink, is now built on servers and connectivity. The new kingdoms are not bound by borders, but by networks. They are global by default and scalable by design. The castles are no longer stone fortresses, they are cloud-based silos of data and control, guarded not by soldiers, but by encryption and automated gatekeeping. These new rulers are not elected, they are followed. Their legitimacy is not won at the ballot box, but through retention metrics and engagement graphs. Influence is not about jurisdiction, it's about reach.

And while the old symbols remain, the flags still wave, the anthems still play, the ceremonies still unfold, the true location of sovereignty has shifted. The nation-state issues the passport, yes. It grants identity in the eyes of customs agents and immigration officers. But the platform determines access. Access to speech, to income, to audience, to tools, to knowledge, to relevance. You may be a citizen in the eyes of the state, but if you are banned by the platform, you are silenced in the modern agora. If you are locked out of the interface, you are locked out of the world.

In this new regime, access is power. Access to platforms is access to speech. Access to payment systems is access to livelihood. Access to networks is access to meaning, movement, and influence. The nation may still command physical loyalty, but the platform commands daily reality.

And so, the wise prince of today must stop thinking in the language of territory and start thinking in the language of protocols. The battleground is no longer the capital, it is the cloud. The gate to power is not the palace, it is the login screen. And the one who controls access controls the world.

VI

Narrative is Sovereignty

The Power to Tell the Story is the Power to Rule. In every age, sovereignty has rested on a singular foundation: the ability to define reality in the minds of others. Power begins not with the sword, the coin, or the law, it begins with the story. In earlier eras, rulers cultivated this power through religion, ritual, and divine right. The pharaoh was a god. The king ruled by heaven's mandate. The emperor's decree was truth because it echoed through temples, cathedrals, and sacred texts. The people did not need to be coerced; they needed to believe.

Today, altars have been replaced by algorithms, the scripture by the scroll. The rituals of power now take place on timelines and feeds. The belief systems are no longer organized by clergy but by influencers, journalists, bots, and platform AIs. But the principle remains unchanged: to rule is to author the dominant narrative. The symbols may evolve, but the game is the same. The sovereign is not the one with the most soldiers, but the one with the most believable story.

This is the first and final lesson for the Prince in the age of technofeudalism: narrative is sovereignty. It is not merely a tactic; it is the terrain itself. If you control the story, you control public perception. If you control perception, you control behavior. And if you control behavior, you control reality. In this world, land, armies, and bureaucracies are relics. The real battleground is the collective imagination. To possess power is to possess narrative infrastructure: the tools, channels, and language through which belief spreads and meaning is manufactured.

You may hold no official office. You may have no army, no budget, no borders. But if your voice shapes the discourse, if your ideas set the tone of the feed, if your memes define the mood, if your messages are echoed, repeated, believed, you are a ruler in all but name. You write the constitution of the mind, line by line, pixel by pixel.

In a society where attention is the most limited resource, visibility is not merely a sign of influence, it is influence. To be seen is to be real. To be repeated is to be validated. To trend is to triumph. Believability has replaced truth as the cornerstone of persuasion. What matters is not whether something is accurate, but whether it feels right, looks right, and spreads fast. The most enduring beliefs are not proven, they are performed, reinforced by social cues, repetition, and emotional resonance.

Thus, the Prince must abandon the notion that truth alone holds power. In the information war, truth is optional, but believability is essential. Legitimacy in the modern age does not emerge from fact, but from frame. Whoever frames the debate wins it. Whoever dictates the question, controls the answer. The ruler of the 21st century is not the keeper of truths, but the architect of perceptions.

This chapter is not a moral treatise. It does not ask whether this world should exist. It asks how one can survive and thrive within it. This is not a call for honesty or ethics, it is a manual for sovereignty in a chaotic, contested attention economy.

We will examine how the battle for control has shifted from borders to feeds, from law to language, from speeches to deepfakes. We will study how narrative is manufactured, how reality is scripted, and how influence is scaled. From the viral meme to the algorithmic echo chamber, from the influencer to the psy-op, we will dissect the modern arsenal of the digital ruler.

And we will chart a path for the Prince, not the righteous prince, not the benevolent prince, but the effective one. The one who knows that in a world of fractured realities, the most powerful weapon is not truth, but belief. And the battlefield is not the land beneath your feet, it is the timeline in your hand.

In this era, control of narrative is control of fate. And the ruler who can write the story writes the world.

The Collapse of Objective Reality

For most of recorded history, rulers understood that the path to lasting control ran not only through armies and treasuries, but through truth, or at least, the appearance of it. Power was not merely enforced; it was believed. Religion, ideology, and law were the great instruments of narrative order. The Church proclaimed divine authority and burned those who spoke otherwise. Monarchs legitimized their thrones through bloodlines and myths of destiny. States printed textbooks and declared which version of history would be taught, remembered, and inherited. These institutions did not simply dictate what could be done, they dictated what was. Reality itself was curated, and often violently protected.

But the digital age has shattered this order. It has obliterated the notion of a single, unifying truth. What once took centuries of theological consensus, bureaucratic approval, or royal decree can now be undone by a single post, a viral clip, or a meme. Reality, once centralized and enforced, is now fragmented, atomized into a million feed-driven universes. Each citizen, scrolling through their personalized interface, experiences a different world. Their perceptions are shaped not by common institutions, but by machine-learning algorithms designed to maximize engagement, not accuracy. The result is a culture in which no two people inhabit exactly the same narrative space.

This is not mere noise or confusion. It is a fundamental rewiring of society's epistemology. There is no longer one shared truth, but a kaleidoscope of overlapping, often contradictory, fictions. There is no longer a single public square, but a thousand gated communities of belief, each with its own idols, dogmas, and heresies. The age of "the truth" has given way to the age of "your truth", a phrase that would have been unthinkable in a medieval court or 20th-century newsroom, but is now accepted, even celebrated.

In such a world, the one who shapes perception holds greater power than the one who commands action. This is the paradox of post-truth governance: people do not act based on reality as it is, but on reality as they believe it to be. A man will not storm a palace because of a budget deficit, but he may do so because of a viral video, a conspiracy theory, or a belief that the system is rigged. He will not change his habits because of climate models, but because a narrative reached him in a form that felt true. To understand this is to understand the new mechanics of control: facts matter less than frameworks. Statistics matter less than stories.

Thus, the sovereign of the digital age must master the narrative domain. He must treat perception as terrain to be mapped, shaped, and defended. The citizen's belief is not a byproduct of power, it is its very foundation. If people believe you are legitimate, you are. If they believe you are corrupt, you are. If they believe someone else offers a more compelling story, then your reign is already over, no matter how many bureaucrats or soldiers you command.

This is the modern ruler's advantage, and his greatest threat. For if he understands narrative, he can rule silently, subtly, invisibly. He can manufacture consent without force, obedience without surveillance. He can guide belief with a hashtag, destabilize rivals with a whisper campaign, or reframe dissent as delusion. But if he fails to understand narrative, if he cedes the story to others, he will watch his authority evaporate in real time, drowned out by a thousand more captivating voices.

Because once the people stop believing your story, you are no longer their Prince. You are just another account, another relic, another voice lost in the feed.

In this fractured world, sovereignty is not written in law. It is told in story. It is remembered in meme. It is shared in screenshot.

And those who rule must become narrators before they can become kings.

Memes, Myths, and Modern Magic

The meme is the modern sigil. It is not a trivial joke or disposable piece of internet detritus, it is a symbol charged with narrative force, a compact spell of persuasion engineered for rapid spread and deep resonance. In an age where information moves faster than armies and where attention is scarcer than gold, the meme has become one of the most potent weapons in the sovereign's arsenal. It is a unit of ideology, a compressed myth, a fragment of narrative that bypasses the rational mind and imprints itself directly onto the nervous system.

Where rulers of the past built temples, pyramids, and palaces to assert their power and permanence, today's rulers build viral content. The monuments of this age are not made of stone, they are made of pixels, timestamps, and reposts. A meme that travels far enough, fast enough, becomes an icon. It imprints itself on the public imagination, distilling complex ideologies, identities, and allegiances into a single image or phrase. One well-timed meme can dismantle a movement, ridicule a politician into irrelevance, or elevate a forgotten outsider into the spotlight of global attention.

This may seem new, but it is simply the newest form of ancient practice. In the past, rulers cloaked themselves in sacred symbols, crowns to signify divine right, regalia to evoke awe, language tailored to impress both peasant and noble alike. Every gesture, every garment, every public appearance was a curated performance meant to reinforce a shared fiction: that the ruler was not just powerful, but rightful, elevated, set apart. These rituals worked not because they were true, but because they were believed. They shaped collective memory, established emotional bonds, and prevented rebellion through the sheer weight of myth.

Today, that same process happens in milliseconds through the feed. Narrative is no longer crafted through cathedral sermons or state-sponsored epics, it emerges through image macros, viral videos, TikTok edits, and tweetstorms. The modern mythology is written in memes. It is coded in the aesthetics of irony, humor, provocation, and familiarity.

The sovereign who understands this does not waste time trying to explain policy or correct misinformation. He creates symbols. He seeds culture. He fights not for facts, but for emotional real estate.

A crown is no longer forged, it is photoshopped. A man's reputation is not earned slowly over decades, it can be built in a weekend with the right combination of narrative, image, and attention. Reality itself is malleable to the meme-maker. A falsehood repeated in the right tone, with the right aesthetic, can gain more traction than a truth spoken plainly. A smear can become a legacy. A joke can become scripture.

Memes are not marginal, they are central. They are not noise, they are signal. In the new attention economy, memes function as banners in a battlefield of belief. They signify allegiance, declare identity, and rally the masses more effectively than any formal speech. They are symbols to be raised, weapons to be deployed, and spells to be cast.

The wise Prince does not dismiss them. He wields them. He understands that every image may be an icon waiting to be born. Every phrase may be a scripture in embryo. Every symbol may become the standard around which an army of minds will rally. He does not merely hope to persuade; he seeks to enchant.

Because in the age of platforms, you are not in competition for reason, you are in competition for belief. And belief is not won with data. It is won with myth, repetition, rhythm, and feeling.

So rule not only with laws, but with sigils. Not only with institutions, but with symbols. And remember: the meme is not trivial. The meme is the myth of now.

The Spectacle is the Sovereign

Political theorist Guy Debord once observed that in societies dominated by modern production, all of life becomes an "immense accumulation of spectacles." That was in 1967, before smartphones, before algorithmic feeds, before dopamine loops engineered by artificial intelligence. Debord described a world in which representation had begun to displace reality, where appearances were no longer reflections of truth, but substitutes for it. He saw early signs of what has now become absolute: the Spectacle is not merely part of life, it is life.

In the current age, we no longer experience the world directly. We experience it through screens, through feeds, through lenses of performance. Reality is not something that unfolds before us; it is something we scroll through, react to, remix, and forget. What once passed for truth, evidence, expertise, experience, has been supplanted by virality. What once defined credibility, accomplishment, knowledge, legacy, has been replaced by influence. The modern sovereign is not the one who speaks softly and governs wisely, but the one who commands the feed and dominates the discourse.

Ask yourself: who holds more power today, the policy analyst drafting regulatory frameworks, or the meme-lord who can make a billion people laugh, sneer, or rage? Who moves the public mind, the career bureaucrat crafting healthcare policy behind closed doors, or the YouTuber who turns a camera, a voice, and a mood into a nationwide movement? In the theater of modern governance, substance is secondary to spectacle. The screen is the throne.

This is not hyperbole. This is structure. In a culture governed by attention, attention is governance. The person who captures the most eyes commands the culture. And culture is not a soft force, it is a regime of norms. It defines what is acceptable, what is moral, what is possible. It shapes the field on which laws are passed, votes are cast, and movements are born. Culture is the invisible architecture of consent. And the architecture is built out of images, loops, soundbites, virals, and spectacles.

Thus, a ruler today must understand the logic of the attention economy with the same urgency and precision that a medieval general understood siegecraft. You are not simply competing for voters, followers, or even believers. You are competing for screen time. If your message does not surface, it does not exist. If your face is not familiar, your rule is not legitimate. If your voice cannot cut through the noise, you are already silenced.

This is why allegiance today is built through aesthetics as much as policy. People do not align with platforms because of spreadsheets or white papers, they align with symbols, sensations, and emotional consistency. Spectacle is not a distraction from politics; it is politics. It is the language through which belief is formed, and authority is maintained. If you cannot produce it, you will be eclipsed by someone who can. And once the spectacle belongs to them, so too does your narrative, your reputation, your power.

This is the harsh reality of contemporary sovereignty: legitimacy now flows from attention, not institutions. Capture attention and you shape identity. Hold attention and you consolidate loyalty. Lose attention and you vanish, forgotten by the feed, replaced by the next spectacle.

And make no mistake: if you do not manufacture spectacle, someone else will. Someone with fewer scruples, a sharper aesthetic, or a more emotionally resonant pitch. They will seize your place in the narrative. They will define your character before you even know you're in a story. They will become the center of gravity, and once they do, you are no longer a ruler. You are a relic.

So let the modern Prince understand in an empire of screens, the battle is not for truth or justice, it is for presence. To rule today is not to command, but to perform. And the ones who master performance are not jesters.

They are kings.

Deepfakes and Digital Prophets

We are entering a new epoch, an era not merely of misinformation or media manipulation, but of synthetic reality. What was once the domain of imagination or dystopian speculation has now become operational. With deepfakes, voice cloning, generative video, and AI-authored speech and prose, it is now possible not just to distort truth, but to forge reality itself. The modern sovereign need not spin a story, he can conjure it. Fabrication is no longer an act of interpretation. It is an act of authorship.

Consider this: your rival appears in a video, calmly confessing to a crime, praising an enemy, or insulting the public. The clip circulates. It outrages, scandalizes, shatters reputations. People protest, journalists react, loyalties shift. By the time it is analyzed, debunked, or retracted, the damage is irreversible. A correction may follow, but it cannot match the virality of the first impression. Perception becomes history. Rebuttal becomes noise.

Now reverse the scenario. Imagine you, the Prince, appearing before your people to deliver a rousing address. But in truth, you are elsewhere. The speech is AI-generated, your likeness synthesized, your voice replicated. And yet, it lands with impact. Each version tailored to its recipient: one message, a thousand formats, each emotionally tuned to its audience's values, fears, and hopes. You have spoken in many tongues without opening your mouth. This is not magic. It is a computation.

This is not the future. It is already here. And it changes everything.

In this new terrain, the battle is not for accuracy, but for plausibility. The sovereign of narrative is no longer the one who speaks truth, it is the one who makes the most convincing fiction first. Velocity is authority. A synthetic claim that travels faster than the truth gains the power of belief before the truth has even begun to be examined. And in a hyper-saturated media environment, where millions of stories compete for limited attention, the contest is not over what happened, it is over what feels like it happened.

Trust, once grounded in verification, now rests on aesthetic coherence. A story that feels true, visually, emotionally, linguistically, will override one that merely is true. If it looks right, sounds right, and arrives at the right moment, it is accepted as truth regardless of its origin. Authenticity is no longer a matter of fact, but of style. Reality itself becomes a curated experience, shaped not by evidence, but by emotional design.

This is dangerous. It undermines journalism, law, science, and memory. It blurs the boundary between event and illusion, between witness and viewer. It corrodes the foundations of trust on which societies depend. The very idea of a shared reality begins to fracture under the pressure of engineered multiplicity.

But for the Prince, for the one who seeks to rule, not merely to observe, this is not merely a threat. It is a strategic terrain. The chaos of synthetic narrative is not something to fear. It is something to master.

The Prince must understand: you do not need to eliminate lies. You need to own the means of their production. You must become fluent in artificial authorship. You must know how to direct algorithms, weaponize aesthetics, and time the release of digital illusions with precision. You must build your own mythologies, not wait for them to form by accident. In this world, controlling perception is no longer a matter of charisma, it is a matter of code.

Mastering this terrain does not mean abandoning truth. It means recognizing that truth alone is no longer enough. It must be framed, stylized, and delivered in a form that competes with the spectacle of the unreal. The Prince must become a sorcerer of signals, a tactician of belief in a world where belief is fluid and facts are late to the battlefield.

This is not cynicism. This is survival.

In the age of algorithmic persuasion, reality is not discovered, it is declared. And only the fastest, the most coherent, the most contagious narratives will endure. So sharpen your message. Train your machine. And understand that in this era, to rule is to render.

Digital Religion and the New Faiths

In centuries past, rulers derived their legitimacy from the heavens. Religion served not just to guide the soul, but to sanctify the throne. Kings ruled by divine right, their authority justified by sacred texts, upheld by rituals, and enforced through spiritual fear. To question the king was to question God. Religion was not merely belief, it was a total framework of reality, purpose, and obedience. It was the narrative architecture of empire.

Today, the holy texts have changed. The rituals are digital. But the function of faith in political life remains. In the absence of shared religion, the modern world has not become less religious, it has become differently religious. The gods have scattered, and in their place stand ideologies and identity narratives, new mythologies for a fractured age. These are the belief systems through which meaning is constructed and legitimacy is claimed. They offer salvation, enemies, origin stories, and moral orders. They are the new faiths. And their altars are algorithmic.

Scroll through any feed and you will see it: every digital movement becomes a kind of cult. Not metaphorically, but structurally. Each has its symbols, hashtags, in-jokes, and style codes. Each has its martyrs, figures canceled, attacked, or silenced, held up as proof of persecution and proof of truth. Each has its rituals, performed through content creation, signal boosting, callouts, and affirmations. Each has its heresies, and heretics, swiftly excommunicated through mass unsubscribes, public denouncements, or algorithmic erasure.

Woke. Anti-woke. Crypto maximalists. Techno-optimists. Red-pilled masculinists. Green-pilled environmental mystics. Conspiracy clusters. Political fandoms. Anons. Incels. Justice warriors. Libertarian utopians. Each speaks in the language of faith. They do not simply argue, they believe. And belief is not negotiated through evidence. It is constructed through story, emotion, and identity.

These movements do not rally around traditional politicians. They are not parties. They are churches. And their leaders are not policymakers, but prophets, those who can decode chaos into coherence. The influencer who "sees through the lies." The podcaster who "speaks truth to power." The billionaire who "dreams beyond the limits." These figures shape mass imagination far more effectively than presidents or senators. They are high priests of narrative, wielding cultural authority that outpaces and often undermines the formal political class.

A wise Prince does not mock these movements. He studies them. He understands their inner logic, their pain points, their myths, and their messiahs. He learns their language, not to flatter them, but to use them. He borrows their symbols, aligns with their causes, amplifies their narratives when it suits him, and, when necessary, creates counter-narratives of his own, myths more powerful, more compelling, more contagious. He does not confront belief with brute force. He does not try to disprove ideology with facts. That is the error of the rationalist. He knows you do not defeat belief with evidence, you defeat it with a stronger belief.

Because faith is not broken by reason. It is replaced. And the Prince who fails to understand this, who believes that statistics, charts, or debate will win hearts, will lose not just the narrative, but the realm. People do not need precision. They need meaning. And in a world of noise, the loudest voice is not always the one that commands, it is the one that makes sense of chaos. The one that makes them feel seen. The one that tells them who they are and what they are fighting for.

In this landscape, ideology is not an accessory to power. It is power's foundation. The Prince must therefore become a narrative engineer, a myth-maker, a symbolic strategist. He must know how to speak not just to the mind, but to the soul, the tribal soul, the memetic soul, the viral soul. He must write doctrines that spread like fire. He must sanctify his cause. He must turn governance into liturgy, policy into prophecy, leadership into legend.

And above all, he must remember;

He who commands belief commands the future.

He who builds the stronger myth wins the war.

The Algorithmic Throne

A new kind of throne has emerged in our time, one not carved from stone or forged in gold but constructed from ranking logic and behavioral data. It does not sit in a palace. It hums inside server racks. Its power is not declared, but executed, automatically, invisibly, constantly. This is the throne of the algorithm.

To rule today is not merely to speak, to command, or even to be seen. It is to be ranked first. For in a world mediated by platforms, visibility is not a public good, it is a private allocation. And the allocator, the true arbiter of presence and absence, is the algorithm. It decides what rises and what sinks. It determines who is relevant and who is forgotten. It is the invisible editor of the public square, the gatekeeper of narrative, the silent Minister of Truth.

He who rules the algorithm rules perception itself. This is the most dangerous and most potent truth of the modern age. You do not need to control armies or parliaments. You need only to control the feed. Because the feed is where the modern subject lives. It is the stream of images, headlines, voices, and symbols that shapes belief, memory, and identity. The feed is the kingdom.

If the algorithm amplifies your message, you exist, magnified, legitimized, repeated until you become truth by repetition alone. If it buries your content, you become irrelevant, your speech unheard, your presence erased not by censorship, but by obscurity. And if it bans you outright, if it deems your content unworthy of circulation or in violation of some opaque rule, you are unpersoned. You are not debated or discredited. You are simply gone.

In such a world, a Prince must court the algorithm as he once courted generals, nobles, or high priests. You must learn its logic, its rituals, its secret language. What does it reward? What patterns does it detect? What behaviors does it privilege? This is not flattery, it is survival. You must master the metrics: watch time, click-through rate, engagement velocity, emotional polarity, audience segmentation. These are no longer marketing tools. They are the new instruments of statecraft.

He who understands these signals does not just play the game, he reshapes the board. To command the algorithm is to command the crowd, because in the platform era, the crowd is the algorithm's effect, not its source. It follows what it is shown. It believes what it repeats. The ruler who aligns with the algorithm rules not by law, but by momentum.

But there is a higher level still.

Why merely appease the algorithm when you could be the algorithm? Why pray to the feed when you could own it? The most powerful sovereign is not the one who posts content, it is the one who hosts the platform. The platform does not argue. It selects. It does not persuade. It prioritizes. It does not speak. It frames the conversation.

If you own the feed, you do not need to win arguments. You curate belief itself. You decide which truths are shown, which lies are buried, which conflicts are inflated, and which causes go viral. You construct the conditions under which opinion is formed. You become the architect of common sense.

In this realm, narrative is infrastructure. Sovereignty is backend access. And power flows not from the throne of a nation, but from the admin dashboard of a platform.

This is the age of soft empires, where code is policy and ranking logic is law.

And so the Prince must evolve.

He must learn not just how to lead people, but how to lead machines that lead people.

Not just how to govern bodies, but how to govern belief.

And he must understand: in the empire of the algorithm, the sovereign is the curator of reality.

Narrative Assassination

In a previous age, a Prince's greatest fear was the dagger in the dark, a blade slipped beneath the ribs by a rival, an assassin, or a traitorous courtier. Power could be lost in a single, silent moment. But today, the dagger has evolved. It is no longer made of steel, but of story. In the age of narrative warfare, you do not need to kill a ruler to destroy him. You only need to brand him.

To be branded is not merely to be criticized. It is to be reduced, to have your complex identity collapsed into a single, emotionally charged label. Traitor. Fascist. Simp. Fraud. Controlled opposition. Coward. These are not policy critiques or ideological positions. They are narrative viruses. Small, contagious symbols that bypass reason and attach directly to the limbic system. They are designed not to persuade, but to infect.

And once they take root, they spread. Repetition is the weapon. A word, a meme, a soundbite, shared enough times, in enough places, by enough voices, achieves a dangerous alchemy: it feels true. The public does not pause to verify, to weigh the evidence, to interrogate the label. They absorb it through sheer exposure. The flood of repetition becomes indistinguishable from consensus. And in the digital realm, perception is often more powerful than proof.

This is the new battlefield. And branding is its primary weapon. In the hands of a skilled propagandist, a label is more deadly than a sword. It can end careers, shatter legitimacy, erase trust, and poison legacy, all without the need for violence or confrontation. A ruler today must not only command armies or manage economies. He must defend his name, because in a culture ruled by symbols, your name is your power.

The wise Prince understands this. He knows that if he does not define himself, his enemies will do it for him. And once they do, once a frame is set and a name is stuck, all other messages pass through it. A "fraud" cannot be taken seriously, no matter how sound his policy. A "coward" cannot rally a people, no matter how brave his actions. A "controlled asset" is distrusted by default, no matter how real his intentions. These labels are traps. They function as narrative handcuffs, reducing every move you make to another proof of the brand.

Thus, narrative positioning becomes a matter of survival. The Prince must be vigilant not only about what he says, but about what is said about him. He must monitor the symbolic terrain constantly. He must know which words are being attached to his name, which memes are gaining traction, which narratives are coalescing. And when necessary, he must strike first, not with denials, but with definition. He must give himself the name before others do. He must tell the story of who he is, and make that story more powerful, more compelling, and more sticky than the stories his enemies will tell.

This is why Machiavelli warned that it is better to be feared than loved. Not because fear is morally superior, but because fear resists rebranding. Love is volatile. It fades, it turns, it can be reinterpreted. But fear, when rooted properly, sticks. It lingers in the background of every interpretation. It frames the ruler as a force, not as a friend. And in the domain of narrative, framing is everything.

In the end, the Prince who does not master his myth becomes the victim of someone else's. He is not defeated by rebellion, but by redefinition. And once redefined, he is no longer a sovereign. He is a symbol, one he does not control.

This is the age of narrative warfare. The blade is language. The battlefield is the feed. The soldiers are influencers, bots, editors, and trolls.

And the crown is not won, it is believed into being.

So define yourself. Dominate your myth.

Or be rewritten by someone who will.

Propaganda in the Age of the Self

In the past, propaganda was a tool wielded by the powerful, a weapon forged in the furnaces of central authority. A king would issue decrees to be read in the public square. A newspaper, backed by party or patron, would print the version of the truth most aligned with the regime's interests. Ministries would manufacture slogans, posters, and broadcasts, directing the emotional currents of a nation from the top down. The goal was persuasion, but the method was command. The ruler spoke, and the subjects listened.

Today, that structure has inverted. Propaganda has been democratized. The platform economy, engineered for virality, fueled by dopamine, and governed by algorithms, has turned every user into a potential broadcaster. But more importantly, it has turned them into voluntary propagandists. No longer must a sovereign fund newspapers or employ artists to spread his myth. The subjects now do it for him, for free.

This is the brilliance, and the horror, of the platform age: the subject becomes the soldier. Millions of people now create, remix, and amplify content that reinforces the sovereign's narrative. They do so not for gold, not for position, but for clout, for digital recognition, for likes, for status within their tribe. They volunteer for the cause, often without even knowing what cause they serve. They attack rivals, elevate allies, and saturate the feed with curated belief. Their loyalty is not enforced by decree, it is enticed by design.

The skilled Prince understands this new terrain. He does not order obedience. He orchestrates virality. He does not argue for his greatness; he engineers a narrative that compels others to proclaim it for him. He introduces symbols, catchphrases, conspiracies, or provocations, tiny narrative seeds, and then steps back. The network does the rest. The story spreads, mutates, gains momentum. Defenders emerge, critics are swarmed, heretics are mocked, and the myth takes root, not because it is imposed, but because it is performed.

This is not the old model of top-down persuasion. It is a viral model of sovereignty. Power is no longer about broadcasting a single message from the center. It is about seeding thousands of messages at the edges and allowing the algorithmic winds to carry them. Control does not come from command. It comes from suggestion, from framing, from resonance, from emotional payloads wrapped in memetic form.

In this structure, the Prince's job is not to defend himself. That would be weak. It would signal insecurity, invite scrutiny. If you must constantly declare your legitimacy, you have already lost it. Instead, the wise ruler lets others speak for him. He lets the network write his scripture, create his gospel, and spread his doctrine in formats optimized for attention. He lets others drag his enemies, mock them, drown them in ridicule, not because they were asked to, but because they feel compelled to. Because the system rewards the performance.

The illusion of destiny is most powerful when it appears organic. A myth is most effective when it is discovered, not delivered. The Prince who understands this does not shout his greatness. He whispers it into the current, cloaked in humor, ambiguity, and metaphor. He creates symbolic cues that others can pick up and amplify. And if he is truly skilled, if he is a master of narrative architecture, then those who spread his myth will believe it was their idea all along.

This is the apex of influence: to direct without appearing to direct, to rule without appearing to rule, to create a story so compelling, so resonating, that people internalize it as their own. Not propaganda in the old sense, but something more insidious, more effective: crowdsourced mythmaking.

This is the new crown. Not worn but believed into existence.

Not declared, but memed into inevitability.

Not printed in official channels but performed in millions of microgestures across the network.

To rule in the platform age is to understand that truth is less powerful than traction, and control is less about command than contagion.

You do not need to force belief.

You simply need to make it go viral.

The Four Pillars of Narrative Rule

To rule the narrative is not merely to tell a story, it is to shape the reality in which others live, act, and believe. In the age of algorithmic visibility and symbolic warfare, storytelling is no longer entertainment or persuasion. It is governance. The sovereign of this era is not the one who commands territory, but the one who commands meaning. And meaning spreads not through complexity, but through clarity, force, and design. To achieve this, the Prince must master four core principles, pillars of memetic sovereignty and narrative domination.

1. Symbolic Compression

The first law of narrative rule is symbolic compression, the ability to distill your entire message into a single, emotionally charged image, phrase, or figure. A flag. A mask. A hashtag. A face. The more complex the world becomes, the more the human mind craves icons. People do not remember essays; they remember emblems. Symbols bypass analytical thought and operate like software updates for belief, they carry vast emotional and ideological payloads in a form that can be recognized at a glance and shared without explanation.

The power of a symbol lies in its efficiency. A well-designed symbol is a Trojan horse: it enters the psyche quickly, carrying with it a hidden narrative. It signals affiliation. It grants meaning. It says who is "us" and who is "them." In the past, sovereigns minted coins with their image, raised standards with their crest, and imposed architecture that reflected divine right. Today, the Prince must learn to mint memes, deploy slogans, and forge digital icons with the same intentionality.

2. Emotional Primacy

The second pillar is emotional primacy. If you want your narrative to be adopted, it must first be felt. Logic does not drive mass belief, emotion does. The human brain is a pattern-seeking, tribe-joining, threat-detecting machine. It justifies beliefs after the fact, not before. The masses are moved not by spreadsheets, but by shame and pride, fear and hope. Your message must provoke feeling before it is subjected to rational scrutiny, because once emotion is engaged, scrutiny often never comes.

This does not mean abandoning truth. It means dressing truth in the armor of affect. Every story must contain a moment of moral impact. Every phrase must be tuned to emotional resonance. You must tap into ancestral instincts: the desire to belong, the fear of betrayal, the thrill of rebellion, the longing for transcendence. The most effective propaganda does not say, "This is true." It whispers, "This feels right." In the attention economy, the message that moves the heart wins long before the mind catches up.

3. Antagonist Clarity

The third principle is antagonist clarity. Every compelling narrative needs a villain. Ambiguity is the death of conviction. Your people cannot rally around your cause if they don't know what threatens it. They must have someone to fear, someone to blame, someone to fight. The more archetypal the enemy, the stronger the cohesion among your followers. A story without an enemy is not a story, it is a lecture. A movement without an enemy is not a movement, it is a hobby.

Your antagonist must be vivid. They must represent more than themselves, they must embody a threat to your values, your identity, your future. They can be real or symbolic. An institution. A rival ideology. A class, a system, a person, a concept. What matters is clarity. The more focused the target, the more energy the movement can generate. It is not cruelty. It is structure. Every myth needs a demon. Every crusade needs a heretic. The Prince who provides one gives his people a purpose, and binds them to himself as the only viable defender.

4. Repetition and Ubiquity

Finally, the fourth pillar: repetition and ubiquity. Your narrative must not only be powerful. It must be everywhere. No idea, however profound, will survive in obscurity. In the battle for belief, the repeated wins over the reasonable. Just as ancient rulers stamped coins with their image and inscribed their titles on monuments, you must inscribe your message on the cultural feed, again and again, across platforms, across formats, across voices.

Repetition is not redundancy, it is ritual. It builds familiarity. It creates the illusion of consensus. It implants belief through sheer presence. To hear something once is to notice it. To hear it five times is to remember it. To hear it a hundred times is to believe it. The message must be memetic: adaptable, re-creatable, remixable, so that others carry it forward on your behalf. Your narrative must be the background music of the age. Omnipresent. Inescapable. Internalized.

Strategic Counsel for the Modern Prince

Now, let us shift from theory to action. A Prince is not merely a thinker of thoughts, but a mover of worlds. He does not simply observe the flow of narrative, he shapes it, engineers it, rides it like a current toward power. Ideas are important, but strategy is essential. In the realm of narrative, presence without architecture is meaningless. To dominate belief, one must not only understand the principles of myth and perception, one must apply them with deliberate force. And so, here are your imperatives, not as vague suggestions, but as commands worthy of a sovereign.

First, abandon the notion of messaging. You are not running a campaign. You are not delivering talking points. You are building a mythology, an entire cosmology of meaning in which you are the gravitational center. Ask not, "What is my slogan?" Ask, "Who am I in the symbolic order?" The most successful figures in today's cultural landscape are not seen as people, but as mythic forces. Elon is not a CEO, he is the archetype of the mad futurist. Kanye is not a musician, he is the wounded prophet. Trump is not a politician, he is the chaos-bringer, the golden idol, the comic villain, the savior, depending on who tells the story. Greta is not an activist, she is the child oracle, the wrath of nature speaking through innocence. These figures transcend fact. They function on a symbolic level. That is your task. Become a figure too large to cancel, too strange to define, too iconic to ignore.

To achieve this, you must control the entry point. The doorway through which people first encounter you will define how they interpret everything that follows. The first impression is not a minor detail, it is the frame for the entire myth. Design it with intent. Curate your aesthetic, your tone, your emotional register. Are you the outsider, the builder, the redeemer, the exile, the king returned? Choose your archetype and design your presence accordingly. In this digital age, identity is not discovered, it is performed. You must control the stage before the show begins.

And yet, control does not always mean speech. One of the most underutilized weapons in narrative warfare is silence. The temptation to respond to every attack, every rumor, every misquote is strong, but dangerous. To respond is often to submit to someone else's frame. The skilled Prince knows that silence, when wielded with intention, creates mystique. It leaves space for speculation. It signals untouchability. Sometimes silence allows a lie to collapse under its own weight, denied the oxygen of reaction. And sometimes, the best response to an attack is not a rebuttal, but the sudden release of a more compelling story elsewhere, a pivot so captivating that attention is pulled away like a magnet snapping from rusted metal.

But silence alone is not enough. You must always maintain narrative sovereignty. That means you are the author of your legend. You do not allow journalists, rivals, or even allies to define your story. You define it, relentlessly, proactively, even in retreat. Even if you lose power, your story must remain intact. Because narrative is not only a tool of dominance, it is your afterlife. Long after your reign ends, your name will persist in the myths others tell. Will you be remembered as a tyrant? A martyr? A visionary misunderstood? A tragic figure undone by betrayal? You must plant the seeds of your own myth now, before others dig your grave with their version.

Lastly, understand that not all truths need to be delivered directly. Sometimes, the most enduring narratives are conveyed through fictional proxies. Story travels faster than sermon. A film, a parable, a character, a short video, a fictional account, these can carry your message without revealing your hand. In times of conflict, subtext becomes a safer and more effective vehicle than direct speech. Your beliefs, your critiques, your vision for the world, embed them in fables. In cinema. In viral short stories. People resist doctrine. They share fiction. A myth dressed in metaphor slips past the guards of reason. It enters the bloodstream of culture through art, humor, emotion, and it cannot be easily killed.

If these strategies are followed with precision and patience, your narrative will not merely be heard, it will be felt, adopted, and eventually believed as obvious truth. That is the final goal: not persuasion, but transformation. Your story becomes the lens through which reality is interpreted. It becomes background noise. Atmosphere. Unquestioned.

You do not want a message.

You want a myth that survives you.

And you want others to carry it, because they believe it was theirs all along.

Final Counsel: You Are the Story

In the end, all rulers become myths. No matter how vast their empire, how numerous their laws, or how meticulous their governance, they are ultimately reduced to stories. History remembers not in details, but in symbols. It files away the complexity and leaves behind the image. Some are enshrined as saviors, guiding lights of progress, symbols of courage, avatars of change. Others are cast as tyrants, monsters in the national psyche, cautionary tales, shadows whispered through generations. But in both cases, their rule ends. Their story does not.

This is the final truth the Prince must understand: you will be mythologized. Whether you rule a platform, a nation, a company, or a movement, your actions will eventually be filtered, simplified, and canonized in some narrative frame. You can no more stop this process than you can stop the sun from setting. The only question is whether you will write the story, or whether others will write it for you.

If you understand this, if you embrace it, you gain something that transcends territory. You gain legacy. And not just legacy in the hollow, ceremonial sense, but legacy as an operating system, a living software that outlasts the body, the brand, even the moment. When you rule the story, you do not merely govern space, you govern time. You bend memory. You shape the future's understanding of the past.

This is the real power in the age of techno-feudalism. The battle is no longer fought merely with ballots or banknotes. It is not a contest of legal codes or land acquisitions. Those are the visible fronts. But the true battlefield, the one that determines all the others, is the domain of belief. And belief is not enforced by law. It is born of narrative.

The story is the throne.

This is why the wise ruler becomes a myth-maker. Not just a leader, but a legend in progress. He curates his image not for attention, but for durability. He chooses symbols that will outlive trends. He makes moves not just for victory, but for meaning. And above all, he tells his story, clearly, early, and often, before it is told about him.

Because if you do not define your myth, your enemies will. They will write your scripture in the margins of ridicule. They will cast you as villain, fool, footnote. They will erase your name, or worse, misremember it. And once their version spreads, it becomes the air people breathe. Myth does not ask for permission. It fills the void.

So do not leave your legacy to chance. Do not trust time to be kind. Write your myth with intent. Engrave it in every move you make. Let it echo in your silence, thunder in your proclamations, shimmer behind your symbols. Craft it not just for now, but for the retelling. Because in the end, only the unforgettable survive the collapse of kingdoms.

And the throne? It is not a chair. It is not a title. It is not a structure of stone or code.

The throne is wherever the story says it is.

Be the one who writes that story.

Or be the one forgotten by it.

VII

Tokenized Loyalty

Coins, Clout, and Contract to Program Allegiance. In the past, loyalty was intimate. It was forged through proximity, through blood, through ritual. A man bent the knee to his liege because of oaths made in candlelight, because his village depended on protection, or because he believed the king had been chosen by God. Loyalty was personal, relational, often sacred. To betray your lord was to betray your name, your people, your soul. Fealty came with honor, and disloyalty came with shame, or the sword.

But the digital age has replaced the personal with the programmable. The intimacy of loyalty has been abstracted, disembodied, and incentivized. We have entered the era of tokenized allegiance, a system in which loyalty is no longer declared, but tracked. No longer sworn, but staked. No longer enforced by honor or fear, but by systems of yield.

In the regime of techno-feudalism, allegiance has been transformed into a transactional and modular experience. It is no longer one oath to one sovereign, but thousands of micro-loyalties, each gamified, measurable, and conditional. The modern subject does not kneel before a king. He follows, subscribes, retweets, pledges, donates. He earns badges. He buys in. He receives access codes, NFT gates, private Discord roles, social tokens, and governance rights. Devotion is rewarded with visibility. Participation is rewarded with yield. Influence is rewarded with more influence. The throne is now a dashboard.

What once required charisma or fear now requires architecture. The new sovereign does not need to be loved. He does not need to inspire awe. He needs only to build the right system, a feedback loop of incentives so seamless that people stay loyal because disloyalty would simply be inefficient. The Prince who understands this shift knows that he no longer needs command. He needs to design. The contract replaces the crown.

Tokens, whether financial, symbolic, or social, are the new lands of fealty. In the old feudal order, land was wealth. Granting land meant creating vassals. In the digital order, attention is wealth, and tokens are the new parcels. A creator's coin, a DAO's token, a platform badge, these are not gimmicks. They are territory. And when you give someone a stake in your tokenized domain, they become your digital vassal. Not through loyalty of the heart, but through the logic of yield.

And yet, this system goes deeper than economics. Because beyond coins lies clout, a more abstract but equally powerful currency. Clout is the social token of the self. People do not just stake money; they stake identity. They project your ideas, your symbols, your language, because it enhances their own standing. They don't merely share, they perform allegiance. In doing so, they build your power while believing they are building their own. This is the brilliance of programmable allegiance: obedience feels like self-expression.

A Prince who masters this terrain can build a kingdom that needs no borders, no army, no flag. He builds a network state of influence, a sovereign territory defined not by land, but by alignment. And that alignment is maintained not by fear or dogma, but by designed incentives, reputation systems, yield farming, subscriber perks, prestige tiers, algorithmic rewards. Loyalty becomes self-reinforcing. Defection becomes socially or economically expensive. And the subjects become enforcers, policing each other, upholding the narrative, defending the sovereign not out of duty, but out of alignment with self-interest.

This is the new face of feudalism. Not castles and kings, but coins and contracts. Not heraldry and bloodlines, but hashtags and badges. The modern sovereign must therefore become not just a ruler, but a protocol designer, an architect of systems that reward belief and penalize deviation. He must see loyalty not as something earned in speech but encoded in the product.

In this world, charisma is secondary. Ideology is optional. What matters is engagement. What matters is building the system in which loyalty feels natural, where participation is its own reward, where allegiance scales, where exit is too costly.

To rule in this age is not to command. It is to design.

To build systems where obedience is gamified, and devotion is profitable.

To create a kingdom where people serve you not because they must, But because they benefit from doing so.

And in that design lies the future of power.

The Token as Feudal Unit

In the medieval world, feudalism was a system of structured dependence, clearly defined by hierarchy, tradition, and transaction. Loyalty flowed upward in exchange for land, protection, and privilege. The peasant owed grain to his lord in return for safety. The knight owed service to his king in return for honor and estate. These obligations were public, ceremonial, and enforced through bloodline and custom. Every subject knew his place, every title had its price, and every allegiance could be traced to material benefit or moral obligation. The chain of loyalty was visible, its links forged from duty, enforced by oaths, and maintained through ritual.

Today, that world is gone, but the logic remains. The castle walls have disappeared, but the structure of fealty has not. It has simply been rendered in new materials, migrated into new domains. The sovereign no longer walks among marble halls, he lives in dashboards and smart contracts. The knight no longer carries a sword, he wields a meme. The peasant no longer tills the land, he posts, likes, shares, and builds engagement.

Where once a Prince bestowed land to create loyalty, today he distributes tokens. These may be literal, cryptographic assets that carry monetary or governance value, or symbolic: exclusive access rights, loyalty points, creator coins, or social badges. Regardless of their form, they serve the same function: they are units of favor. Instruments of alignment. And like land in the old world, they can be given, sold, inherited, or revoked.

Where once a banner or sigil conferred identity, today that mark of belonging appears as a profile badge, a username flare, a special role in a private community. Digital heraldry. And just as the knight once rode into battle bearing the colors of his house, so too does the modern user brand himself with affiliations, flags not of geography, but of ideology, fandom, or protocol. These symbols do not merely reflect allegiance; they reinforce it. They are performed and displayed, curated and guarded, shared with pride or shame, depending on the community they serve.

Access, too, has been transformed. The throne room is now a Discord server, a private Telegram channel, a token-gated livestream. Once, only the favored could enter the court and whisper in the ruler's ear. Now, access is programmable. Tiered. Monetized. One token might allow entrance to the inner circle. Another may allow a vote. Another, the right to speak. These privileges are no longer handed out through bloodline or birthright, but through staking, subscribing, and signaling. The court is still exclusive, but now it runs on scripts, smart contracts, and APIs.

And reputation, which once was earned through battle, conquest, or loyal service, is now tallied in follower counts, engagement metrics, and clout scores. The knight's record of valor has become the verified checkmark. The feat of arms has become a viral tweet. The path to honor is not through combat, it is through visibility. The algorithm is now the battlefield. And victory belongs to those who can win the war of attention.

At the center of all this lies the token, whether fungible or not, whether economic or symbolic. It is the basic unit of modern fealty. It signals access, status, alignment. It can be wielded as a weapon or offered as a reward. It is portable, programmable, and deeply social. Its value is not merely what it can buy, but what it represents. To hold a token is to say: I belong. I believe. I serve. The token binds the user to the platform, the fan to the creator, the citizen to the protocol, the subject to the sovereign.

And the genius, or the danger, of this system is that it does not demand obedience. It does not require enforcement. In most cases, the subject binds himself willingly. He pledges not under duress, but under delight. He sees benefit. He feels like he belongs. He is rewarded for his loyalty not with bread or security, but with social capital, with early access, with governance rights, with public recognition. The system does not need to threaten him. It merely needs to reward him enough to stay. It transforms loyalty from a duty into a game, and the subject plays eagerly, thinking it is freedom.

This is the new feudalism. It is not a regression. It is an evolution. A distributed, algorithmic, tokenized fealty that scales across continents and protocols. And the modern Prince, if he is wise, does not resist it. He masters it. He learns to mint allegiance. To architect prestige. To convert identity into infrastructure.

For the throne is no longer made of stone.

It is made of code, clout, and commitment, staked not in blood, but in tokens.

Loyalty Without Ideology

Traditional rulers understood that to govern the many, they needed more than laws or weapons, they needed belief. Faith was the great binding force of civilization. Religion, nationalism, ideology: these were the invisible threads that wove disparate people into a coherent whole. Belief gave legitimacy to power, sacredness to hierarchy, and purpose to sacrifice. A citizen might suffer for his king if he believed the king was appointed by God. A soldier might die for his flag if he believed it stood for something larger than himself. A worker might toil in hardship if he believed in the promise of revolution. Belief was the alchemy that turned crowds into nations and rulers into symbols.

But in the tokenized age, belief has become optional. It is no longer the prerequisite for loyalty. In a world of programmable incentives and decentralized platforms, engagement has taken the place of faith. Loyalty, once rooted in conviction, is now rooted in calculation.

This is the subtle genius of modern systems: they do not require the heart; they only require behavior. A follower does not need to love you, trust you, or even agree with you. He needs only to receive something of value: status, entertainment, access, yield. If these rewards are designed well, if they are consistent, scalable, and visible, then loyalty emerges as a byproduct. Not out of moral duty, but out of rational alignment. You do not need to command belief. You need only to make participation rewarding.

Take, for example, a Twitch streamer. His subscribers may know little about his ethics or beliefs. They may not care. What they care about is the reward: the entertainment of the stream, the dopamine rush of interaction, the badge that marks them as insiders, the chance to win a giveaway or have their name read aloud. The loyalty shown is not ideological. It is transactional. But it feels real. And, for the purpose of the system, it functions.

Or consider a contributor to a DAO, a decentralized autonomous organization. He may not admire the project's founders or resonate with its stated mission. But he holds governance tokens. Those tokens have value. That value depends on the health of the ecosystem. Therefore, he contributes, promotes, and defends the project, not because he believes in it, but because his self-interest is staked in its success. Loyalty is no longer a question of emotion. It is a question of mechanics.

This is what makes tokenized loyalty so powerful, and so potentially dangerous. It is more durable than belief, because it is not based on sentiment. It is based on incentive architecture. It does not rise and fall with scandals, contradictions, or moral ambiguity. A political figure, religious leader, or ideological movement can collapse in the face of hypocrisy. But a tokenized system can survive contradiction, so long as it continues to pay.

As long as the token yields value, the allegiance holds.

The implication for the modern Prince is profound. In this landscape, preaching values is no longer the most effective path to power. Values may attract attention, but they are fragile. They must be defended, justified, explained. They are vulnerable to shifts in public mood. But incentives, if properly constructed, engineer behavior directly. They bypass belief and go straight to the nervous system. The Prince must therefore become an architect of systems, not a preacher, but a programmer. His success depends not on whether the people believe in him, but on whether they continue to act in ways that uphold his rule.

Thus, the question of modern governance becomes: Can you make it rewarding to align with you? Can you create a structure in which people benefit from your success, such that their loyalty becomes self-sustaining? Can you make defection not immoral, but irrational?

The loyalty of belief is poetic.

But the loyalty of incentive is predictable.

It can be modeled. It can be scaled. It can be automated.

And in a world of collapsing ideologies and fragmented attention, that is the true crown.

Programmable Allegiance

In the age of programmable media and decentralized networks, a new form of power has emerged, one that requires neither constant presence nor charismatic persuasion. Through smart contracts, gamified platforms, and incentive-based ecosystems, the modern sovereign can now automate allegiance. No longer must he coax devotion from the crowd. Instead, he architects it. Loyalty becomes not a matter of inspiration, but of design, a preconfigured behavior loop encoded in tokens, rankings, and privileges.

This shift marks the evolution of power from performance to protocol. With the right system in place, a ruler no longer needs to watch over his subjects. The system watches for him. Rewards are distributed, ranks are assigned, access is granted or denied, not by decree, but by rules embedded in code. The subject becomes a player, the sovereign becomes a designer, and the game itself becomes the court.

One such architecture of allegiance can be seen in platforms that require users to stake tokens in exchange for access. Friend.tech, token-gated DAOs, and similar platforms use staking not only as a technical barrier but as a symbolic gesture: to gain entry, one must first show commitment. The more a user stakes, the higher their visibility, privileges, or influence within the network. This mirrors the medieval practice of purchasing one's way into court or offering tribute to demonstrate loyalty. The sovereign does not need to measure the sincerity of allegiance, the mechanism does it for him. Commitment is quantified and rewarded. Rank is no longer conferred by favor, but by investment.

Another model has emerged through on-chain reputation protocols. In various Web3 ecosystems, a user's past behavior, recorded immutably through wallet activity, governance participation, and community contribution, determines their standing. The system calculates a kind of reputational gravity, pulling loyal and active users closer to the center of influence. Privileges such as voting power, access to private groups, or eligibility for rewards are doled out not based on opinion, but on verifiable contribution. The result is a meritocratic nobility, status not inherited, but earned through action, visible to all, impossible to forge.

Yet another layer of allegiance has surfaced in the form of creator coins and social tokens. Platforms like Rally and BitClout allow individuals, especially public figures, creators, and influencers, to mint their own economies. Holding someone's token becomes a proxy for loyalty, fandom, or belief. The more of a sovereign's token you hold, the closer you sit to their inner circle. Proximity is tokenized. Influence is monetized. Those who invest are rewarded not only with economic upside but with access: early content, private channels, decision-making power. What once existed as informal clout now exists as programmable status. And a truly strategic ruler could expand this model, designing a token not just as a currency, but as a vehicle of narrative alignment, where users are literally invested in the sovereign's story and incentivized to spread, defend, and amplify it.

The brilliance of these systems lies in their scalability and self-enforcement. Traditional power structures required watchmen, informants, punishments, and rituals. These new architectures require only code and belief in the code. Allegiance is engineered at the system level. Loyalty is embedded in the structure itself. Behavior is guided not by external authority, but by internal alignment, what appears as freedom is simply well-structured incentives doing their work.

This is the promise, and the peril, of programmable allegiance. It does not ask for love. It does not require fear. It only needs participation. A sovereign who understands this shift can build an empire of influence where the rituals of loyalty are performed daily, voluntarily, and enthusiastically, through staking, voting, contributing, posting, and holding.

The Prince of this age does not rule with speeches.

He rules with systems.

And his power is not in the stories he tells, but in the design of the world in which those stories are rewarded.

Scarcity, Status, and Psychological Control

Tokenized loyalty systems are not merely innovations in technology, they are evolutions in the manipulation of ancient human instincts. Beneath the dashboards and smart contracts lie the same primal drives that once compelled men to kneel before thrones, march under banners, and kill for gods: the desire for status, belonging, exclusivity, and progress. What was once controlled through religion, bloodlines, or ideology is now governed by interface and game design. The modern Prince need not command obedience or inspire faith, he need only understand the psychology of engagement and wrap it in a system that rewards action.

Scarcity is among the oldest forces in the human psyche. We desire what is rare, not because it is necessarily useful, but because it is difficult to obtain. In the old world, sacred artifacts, noble titles, or access to court were precious precisely because few possessed them. Today, that logic still holds. A badge on a profile, an exclusive NFT, a token-gated Discord room, these are not simply rewards; they are symbols of distinction. When access is limited, it becomes valuable. When a role is hard to achieve, it becomes revered. The Prince who understands scarcity, does not simply distribute rewards, he crafts mythologies of access. What is rare becomes sacred. What is abundant becomes invisible.

Equally powerful is the mechanism of progression. Human beings are wired to crave movement, advancement, the feeling that one's efforts are leading somewhere. This drive has been exploited by both religions and RPGs, confession for spiritual XP, quests for gear upgrades. In the digital kingdom, the sovereign must harness the same architecture. Tiers of loyalty, visible ladders from outsider to insider, from acolyte to knight, create aspiration. Levels, streaks, and rank systems motivate users to act not out of obligation, but out of an intrinsic desire to grow. Loyalty becomes a journey, and the user becomes the hero of their own tale, scripted, of course, by the sovereign's design.

Recognition, though subtle, is just as potent. Human beings are social creatures; we crave acknowledgment. To be seen, to be named, to be called out, these are not mere gestures. They are currency. A like, a mention, a role granted publicly, these convert anonymous followers into evangelists. The sovereign's attention becomes a kind of divine favor. It need not be frequent. In fact, the rarer it is, the more valuable it becomes. The architecture must be designed so that recognition is earned, and when it is given, it transforms the subject into a zealot, not out of fear, not out of love, but because they have been seen by the source of narrative gravity.

Exclusivity is another essential lever. When everyone is allowed in, no one feels chosen. When access must be earned, it becomes precious. The Prince must create not just systems of inclusion, but layers of exclusion. Let the outer ring crave the inner sanctum. Let the plebeian dream of becoming a patrician. The architecture should lock privileges behind thresholds, not to punish, but to create hunger. Privilege, when visible, fuels ambition. When users know that more access, more influence, or more intimacy with the sovereign lies just beyond the next tier, they will climb, and pay, to reach it.

But perhaps the deepest and most binding force is the sense of belonging. When a user begins to identify not just with the sovereign, but with the community built around him, loyalty transforms from transaction to identity. Rituals, inside jokes, shared language, mutual enemies, these cultural markers make a group feel at home. And once a user internalizes that identity, leaving becomes psychologically expensive. They are no longer just supporting a project; they are defending themselves. The boundary between belief and self blurs. Loyalty becomes not a behavior, but a form of existence.

All of this culminates in a new mode of rule, one that does not require charisma, violence, or moral authority. The modern Prince governs not through love or fear, but through systems. Progress bars, token burns, Discord emojis, and tiered access take the place of swords and sermons. Fealty is no longer declared; it is demonstrated through engagement metrics. The sovereign becomes not a speaker, but a designer of loops. Not a king, but a game master.

In this model, power is not performed. It is encoded. The sovereign rules not by standing above the people, but by building the lattice in which they move, grow, and belong. Loyalty is not extracted, it is generated, mechanically and emotionally, until it becomes indistinguishable from free will.

And so, the Prince must not ask how to be loved, feared, or obeyed.

He must ask: How do I design the world in which people reward themselves for serving me?

That is modern sovereignty.

Not command.

Not coercion.

But code that compels allegiance through the architecture of desire.

Gamification as Governance

In the age of techno-feudalism, governance has undergone a quiet but radical transformation. It is no longer enforced by threat or reinforced by moral authority; it is designed. The Prince no longer needs to discipline his subjects with decrees or violence. He needs only to construct a system where desired behavior is the most rewarding behavior. In this regime, obedience is not demanded. It is incentivized.

This is an essential shift from law to logic. Traditional governance relied on laws: clear, top-down commands that drew boundaries and imposed punishments. "Do not speak against the crown," said the sovereign, and failure to comply might result in exile, imprisonment, or execution. This model required force. It required oversight, enforcers, surveillance. It was loud, visible, and costly.

But in the algorithmic order, the Prince no longer needs to outlaw dissent. He need only reward alignment. Instead of saying, "Do not speak against me," he builds a system that says, "If you speak in my favor, you will be elevated, seen, and enriched." The outcome is the same, compliance, but the path to it is quieter, more elegant, and far more effective. Because when power is distributed through rewards, people comply voluntarily. There is no need for police. The system polices itself. The subject becomes his own censor, his own propagandist, his own warden.

We see this logic at work all around us. Consider the architecture of platforms like Reddit, Twitter, TikTok, or Uber. These systems do not simply deliver services, they train behavior. Reddit's karma system nudges users to say what earns upvotes. Twitter's blue check creates hierarchies of legitimacy and subtly punishes the unverified. TikTok's

- TOKENIZED LOYALTY

For You Page promotes content that triggers high engagement, ensuring that creators, over time, learn to optimize their voice, their format, their message to feed the algorithm's preferences. Uber's star ratings teach both drivers and riders how to perform politeness, patience, and conformity. These features may appear innocuous, but they are in fact governance protocols. They establish expectations, incentivize conformity, and gradually suppress anything that does not align with the logic of the system.

In this environment, the Prince does not rule with fear. He rules with feedback. He does not threaten punishment. He offers reputation. He does not jail the dissenter. He simply ensures the dissenter is unseen, unheard, unfavored by the algorithmic gods. And most critically, the Prince does not even need to distribute these rewards himself. He lets the appearance of reward do the work.

This is where the real genius of system-level governance reveals itself. The sovereign allows his subjects to compete for proximity, attention, status, and tokenized value. They vie for his favor not because they are commanded to, but because the structure of the game compels it. Each post, each comment, each contribution becomes a move in a tournament where the prizes are recognition, access, yield, or even just symbolic affiliation. The subjects do not feel governed. They feel engaged. But their engagement serves the ruler. They enforce norms, amplify the narrative, and filter out dissent, all in the hope of reward, or even just the possibility of reward.

Governance becomes a game. Reputation becomes the leash. And the Prince, instead of issuing laws, writes the rules of the system. He designs the tournament. He sets the incentives. And then he lets the crowd do the rest. This form of rule is not only more stable, but also more scalable. Because when a population governs itself through its own desire for visibility, favor, and gain, the sovereign has already won.

To rule in this new age is not to command.

It is to construct the scoreboard.

It is to build a world in which loyalty looks like winning, and deviation looks like failure.

Not because you say so.

But because the system does.

The Emergence of Digital Nobility

Every feudal system, whether ancient or algorithmic, eventually gives rise to a class of enforcers. These are not simply followers or citizens, they are stakeholders, the privileged few who have secured their position closest to the sovereign flame. In medieval courts, they were barons and dukes, lords of land and sword, whose fortunes depended on the favor of the king. In today's digital principalities, they appear in different forms: moderators with banhammers, whales with oversized token holdings, influencers with algorithmic reach, early investors with governance rights, or simply power users who know how to work the system better than the masses they stand above.

These individuals are more than loyalists. They are extensions of the sovereign's will. They enforce the culture, shape the discourse, and defend the architecture of power not out of idealism, but out of alignment. Their interests have been braided into the system. Their influence is derived from their proximity to the throne. And so, when they act, they act not only for themselves, but for the continuation of the order that privileges them.

Their functions are both obvious and subtle. On the surface, they serve as gatekeepers. They guard the inner sanctum of the platform, community, or protocol. They know the rituals, enforce the norms, identify intruders, and swiftly punish dissent. Sometimes they do this through formal authority, admin roles, moderation privileges, voting rights. More often, they do it through cultural policing: mockery, exclusion, shadowbanning, or flooding dissent with algorithmic noise. They create an environment where the feel of consensus is enforced, even if no decree is ever issued.

TOKENIZED LOYALTY

But these nobles are also evangelists. Their status depends on the perceived greatness of the sovereign and the health of his myth. Therefore, they preach. They amplify the message, spread the gospel, correct the narrative, and punish heresy. They are not paid to do this, in many cases, they volunteer, but they are rewarded in more powerful currencies: attention, prestige, access, and future upside. The more they support the sovereign, the more the system supports them.

And perhaps most importantly, they act as guardians of capital. If the sovereign has issued tokens, whether social, financial, or symbolic, these enforcers are its fiercest defenders. Not because they are loyal out of emotion, but because they are financially entangled. They have skin in the game. Their bags are full. And when the token is attacked, be it through criticism, competing narratives, or signs of instability, they rise not as volunteers, but as invested nobles defending the value of their holdings. They will fight to protect the narrative because the narrative protects their wealth.

But with power comes danger. These individuals are necessary to rule at scale, but they are also potential threats. If given too much autonomy, they may begin to believe their influence is their own, not borrowed, not conditional, but inherent. And when that happens, the Prince may find himself surrounded not by loyal nobles, but by would-be kings. Conversely, if these agents are underfed, given too little status, too little access, too little reward, they will drift. They will defect. They will migrate toward rival sovereignties that promise better yields, more prestige, or a more fertile myth to believe in.

Therefore, the Prince must master the delicate art of balancing status with dependence. He must reward these nobles well, but never completely. Give them enough to feel powerful, but not enough to act independently. Allow them to bask in prestige, but remind them, quietly and constantly, that their light comes from the crown. The moment they forget that, the moment they believe their power is natural or self-sustaining, the risk of insurrection begins.

To govern in the digital feudal order is not simply to manage the masses, it is to manage the managers. To cultivate an elite that is loyal, capable, ambitious, and dependent. Too ambitious, and they become dangerous. Too content, and they become complacent. The sovereign must always keep them slightly hungry, close enough to feel chosen, far enough to feel indebted.

This is not cruelty. It is structure. The court must orbit the throne, not escape its gravity.

And so, the Prince does not rule alone. He rules through his network of enforcers, evangelists, and loyalists, so long as they remember that their privilege is not theirs by right, but by favor.

Power flows downward.

But it must also remind itself, at every level, where it comes from.

The Peasantry of the Feed

Not all users are nobles. In fact, most are not. The vast majority of participants in the digital realm occupy a different position entirely, they are serfs of the algorithm. They do not hold governance tokens, nor wield influence, nor shape the narrative directly. They scroll. They watch. They click. They comment. They produce the very lifeblood of the system, data, while understanding little of the system's architecture. Their labor is not in policy or platform design, but in perpetual engagement. They chase likes, crave replies, seek followers, and pour their time into short-form expressions of identity and desire. But they do so within invisible enclosures, digital fiefdoms whose borders they neither drew nor control.

These peasants, unlike the nobles, do not need deep systems of access or status management. They can be ruled en masse through simplified tokens of engagement: the heart, the upvote, the follow, the ping of a notification. What they require is not complexity, but stimulation. Emotion, drama, tribal identity, and fleeting recognition, these are the mechanisms by which their attention is harvested and their allegiance retained. They do not demand governance rights; they demand content. They are governed not by law or tokenomics, but by the rhythm of the feed.

The Prince must learn to see this population not as individuals to persuade, but as an attention commons, a vast, shifting field of cognitive energy that can be cultivated, extracted, and redirected. These users produce narrative power simply by participating, by reacting, sharing, commenting, simping, fighting. Their behavior generates signal. Their volatility becomes trend. Their passions create momentum. But they are not the architects of these dynamics, they are the soil in which others plant.

To rule this class, one does not need to win their hearts in any enduring sense. One must only own the systems that direct their attention. That means owning, influencing, or optimizing the algorithms that determine what they see, when they see it, and how it makes them feel. If the sovereign cannot directly command their belief, he must at least shape the conditions under which belief emerges. His power lies not in universal admiration, but in strategic placement, to ensure that his content, his symbols, his myths occupy the top of their feeds, the center of their discourse, the background noise of their scrolling.

And this is where the nobles come in. The moderators, influencers, and loyal stakeholders who farm engagement at scale, they are the stewards of the serfs. The Prince need not speak to the crowd directly. He must only ensure that his emissaries, his evangelists, his memetic shock troops are properly incentivized and visible. Let them spark the drama, trigger the emotion, manufacture the spectacle. The peasants will respond as they always have by feeding the machine.

In return, the serfs must be given just enough to feel involved. A retweet, a reply, a shoutout from someone above them in the hierarchy. A badge, a shareable moment, a chance to trend for a second. They do not need autonomy. They need spectacle. A continuous stream of narrative that confirms their identity, inflames their passions, and rewards their behavior with ephemeral status. That is what keeps them locked in. That is what keeps them working.

And when managed well, this dynamic becomes self-sustaining. The attention they give becomes data. The data feeds the algorithm. The algorithm favors those aligned with the sovereign. The sovereign's message spreads. The message becomes culture. Culture becomes power.

Thus, the Prince must never mistake the masses for co-authors of the realm. They are its energy source. Its ambient noise. Its mirror. The wise ruler harvests them not with promises, but with frictionless entertainment. He gives them the illusion of proximity, of choice, of relevance. But he never relinquishes control over the stage on which they perform.

Because in this new feudalism, the serfs do not farm land.

They farm attention.

And the harvest flows upward, to whoever owns the feed.

The DAO as Feudal Court

Imagine a medieval village where, instead of a king, all the villagers get a vote on what to build next, a bridge, a wall, a market. But instead of shouting their opinions in the town square, they use tokens to vote digitally, and once the decision is made, a magical machine (smart contract) immediately hires the builder and pays them, no middleman, no arguments.

Now imagine that this system runs 24/7, can be accessed globally, and is open to anyone with an internet connection. That's a Decentralized Autonomous Organization, or DAO. They are often celebrated as the future of egalitarian governance. They are heralded as technological expressions of collective will, liberated from hierarchies, and driven by code rather than charisma. But beneath the surface of decentralization lies a structure that, in practice, resembles something far more ancient: the feudal court.

In a DAO, token holders are the new nobility. Their influence is not distributed equally, but proportionally, measured in stake, not status as a citizen. Those with more tokens wield more power. Their votes carry weight not because of merit or reason, but because of possession. This is not democracy in the classical sense. It is a hierarchy of capital, dressed in the language of participation. Each vote is a reflection of holdings, not a person. This alone echoes the logic of landowning lords in the feudal age, power derives from what one owns, and ownership determines one's voice.

Proposals within a DAO mimic the old custom of court petitioning. Anyone may bring a proposal, just as any subject might request an audience. But not all proposals are heard equally. Some are ignored. Others are quietly buried. And only a few, backed by significant holders or influential voices, rise to the level of community-wide attention. The throne may be theoretically empty, but access to it is still managed by invisible layers of social capital.

And even in the most "decentralized" DAO, the founders remain central figures. Their roles may be formally dissolved, their multisig keys burned, but their influence often lingers like incense in a cathedral. Their early decisions, their cultural framing, their social presence, all act as forms of soft power. Their reputation becomes the architecture. Their early narrative decisions become the mythos that holds the protocol together. The DAO may vote, but the founder's ghost often hovers just above the ballot box.

In this context, the modern Prince must move with subtlety. He must appear democratic while remaining the gravitational center of loyalty, coherence, and vision. Power is no longer seized through fiat. It is maintained through framing. Let the people vote but control the narrative that surrounds the vote. Allow others to execute but be the one who defines what execution looks like, what success means, what values are worth pursuing. Let rewards be distributed broadly but ensure that your own position remains symbolically unshakable. The illusion of distribution is often more effective than distribution itself, especially when the population feels involved.

DAOs, in their most effective form, do not eliminate sovereignty, they mask it. They wrap it in rituals of consensus. They create the sensation of agency, of self-governance, of collective wisdom. But behind every DAO that endures is a story, a figure, a center of gravity. Someone, or something, holding the symbolic crown.

The wise sovereign understands this. He does not resist the DAO. He uses it. He builds systems where the subject feels sovereign, where every proposal feels like empowerment, where every vote feels like freedom. And yet, through influence, incentive design, and strategic silence, the Prince remains the voice they trust, the hand they wait for, the figure they follow.

Let them feel heard. Let them cast tokens like nobles once they cast their support.

But always ensure you are the one whispering in their ear, the one who defines the options, the one who interprets the outcome, the one whose absence would fracture the kingdom.

In the end, decentralization is not the death of rule. It is simply its evolution, rule by narrative, by presence, by consensus manufactured through the subtle machinery of influence.

And so, the throne remains. But now it is made of code, and it moves with you.

Loyalty Farming and Exit Strategies

Tokenized loyalty is one of the most potent tools in the arsenal of the modern Prince. It allows allegiance to be scaled, measured, and monetized. It transforms engagement into currency, and belief into a self-reinforcing system of rewards. But as powerful as this system is, it is also fragile, its strength lies entirely in perception. The illusion must hold. The machine must keep humming. The value must feel real. Because once that perception begins to fracture, once the token falls, the narrative unravels, or the infrastructure fails, the entire structure of loyalty can collapse overnight.

TOKENIZED LOYALTY

The first vulnerability lies in the value of the token itself. Tokenized loyalty depends on the idea that the reward has future potential, that it means something, will grow, or can be exchanged. But if the token's value crashes, either economically or symbolically, the system loses its gravitational pull. Users stop staking. Participants stop contributing. The nobles begin to defect, and the serfs lose interest. It becomes a barren field. To guard against this, the Prince must treat the token not simply as a currency, but as an object of mystique. Scarcity must be preserved. Demand must be engineered. The narrative of value must be refreshed constantly, even artificially. Once a token is seen as worthless, it is almost impossible to recover its aura.

Yet even if the token holds value, the narrative must remain intact. This is the second point of failure: narrative collapse. If the story behind the token, its purpose, its myth, its connection to the sovereign, becomes compromised, no incentive structure can hold the kingdom together. Incentives alone are not enough. People must feel that they are participating in something meaningful, something coherent, something bigger than themselves. When scandals hit, when the leader is disgraced, when the mythology breaks, the incentive system can rot from within. For this reason, the Prince must remain the master of the narrative. He must be vigilant about framing, about symbols, about the tone and tempo of the myth. The token is only as strong as the story that supports it.

There is also the hidden threat of platform dependency. Many tokenized loyalty systems rely on third-party platforms to function, YouTube, Discord, X (formerly Twitter), Patreon, Substack, or countless others. These platforms are not neutral ground. They are sovereign kingdoms in their own right, with their own policies, risks, and agendas. If the Prince builds his loyalty architecture within their walls, he must accept that it can be revoked, demonetized, or banned without warning. A community built entirely on Discord can be cut off with a single TOS violation. A token that relies on Twitter for visibility can vanish when the algorithm shifts. The wise Prince, therefore, must not confuse borrowed infrastructure with true sovereignty. Wherever possible, he must build independent channels, email lists, on-chain communities, self-hosted forums, proprietary apps. The throne must not sit on rented land.

But even with all systems intact, one final threat looms: over-farming. The Prince must never forget that loyalty is a renewable resource, but not an infinite one. If the system extracts too much attention, too much labor, or too much capital from the subjects without adequate reinvestment, the soil will dry. People burn out. Enthusiasm fades. The illusion of fairness disintegrates. Even the most devoted followers will turn cynical if they begin to feel used. For this reason, incentive systems must feel balanced, even if they are strategically rigged in the Prince's favor. The serfs must believe they are winning, or might win, or at the very least that they are seen.

To manage this balance, the Prince must become a designer of cycles. He must learn to refresh the game. Introduce seasonal resets. Create new classes of tokens. Shift the tiers. Add new layers of progression. Remove old ones. He must keep the experience alive and in motion. The loyalty system must feel dynamic, evolving, unpredictable, but fair enough to keep hope alive. The sovereign must take lessons not from governments, but from casinos. In the casino, the house always wins, but the guest always feels like he might.

This is the art of maintaining tokenized allegiance. It is not simply economic or technological. It is theatrical. Psychological. Ritualized. A dance of value and story, perception and reward. And the moment the dance stops, the moment the value feels fake, the story feels broken, the rewards feel stale, the crowd will disperse.

The Prince must therefore be not only a ruler, but a showman. Not only an economist, but a myth-maker. And not only a builder of systems, but a gardener of perception.

Because in the end, tokenized loyalty is not truly about tokens.

It is about the belief that there is still something worth believing in.

Final Counsel: Rule by Reward

We end with this final counsel.

The throne no longer rests above the people, raised on marble steps, separated by ceremony and guarded by steel. It no longer towers from a palace, casting commands down upon a passive population. That image is gone, a relic of a slower world. In this new order, the throne does not loom. It connects. It sits quietly, invisibly, at the center of the network.

And those who sit upon it do not rule by decree. They do not shout their will across public squares or etch their laws in stone. Instead, they design. They build systems. They write rules into code, not constitutions. They govern not through force, but through feedback loops. Through incentives so well-crafted that obedience feels like ambition, and loyalty feels like personal gain.

The modern sovereign mints tokens instead of titles. He grants access instead of privilege. He distributes badges that signal status, gate entry to inner circles, and quietly stratify the social terrain. He builds advancement ladders, not through policy, but through progression mechanics. Levels. Roles. Tiers. Followers. He gamifies his persona until proximity to his name becomes its own form of currency. His court is not a room of nobles, it is a leaderboard. His realm is not a country, it is a culture. And his subjects do not serve him by law, but by playing the game he has designed.

This is not a betrayal of sovereignty. It is its evolution.

To rule in the age of techno-feudalism is not to demand loyalty. It is to create conditions where loyalty becomes the most rational choice, not because of coercion, but because the structure makes alignment profitable. A subject stays not because he is commanded to, but because to leave would mean losing clout, access, status, and identity. The Prince does not ask for love. He creates loops that reward belief. He builds realms of value in which belief becomes self-reinforcing.

And in this system, everything that once symbolized allegiance is reinterpreted in digital form. Tokens are no longer mere financial instruments, they are titles, proof of rank and contribution. A follow is not just a gesture of interest, it is an act of fealty, a signal of submission to a worldview or figure. Access becomes the new currency of affection, those who are closer to the sovereign, or admitted into private channels, feel chosen. Engagement is the new economy, the raw material from which visibility, influence, and revenue are minted. And clout, that nebulous but potent force, is the modern crown. It sits on the head not of the most moral, the most expert, or even the most popular, but of the one who knows how to engineer belief at scale.

So, remember this: rule by reward. Architect systems where status flows upward, where participation becomes ritual, and where loyalty feels like a path to self-actualization. Let your power be felt not in force, but in framework. Govern not by controlling people, but by owning the rules they live by.

Design the system.

Embed the myth.

Reward the allegiance.

Control the center.

Because in this world, he who owns the token, owns the throne.

VIII

Excommunication in the Cloud

Digital Banishment, Censorship, and Algorithmic Erasure. To be silenced is no longer a symbolic loss. It is a sentence. To be erased is no longer a metaphor. It is a death. To be deplatformed is no longer an inconvenience. It is a form of modern excommunication.

In the medieval world, particularly within Christendom, excommunication was not merely a religious penalty. It was the total revocation of visibility, legitimacy, and protection. A man cast out from the Church was not just barred from the sacraments, he was cut off from the world. His legal rights dissolved. His contracts lost their sanctity. His allies, fearing association, abandoned him. His name became a kind of rot, something to avoid, something dangerous to repeat. And most devastating of all, this was not always accompanied by violence. It did not need to be. A single pronouncement could render someone untouchable.

Today, the Church no longer holds that power. But the architecture of excommunication remains. It has been rebuilt, line by line, in the medium of code and algorithm. It no longer wears the robes of religion. It wears the skin of platform policy. Its cathedrals are clouds. Its sacraments are Terms of Service. Its priests are trust-and-safety teams, moderators, algorithmic models that decide, silently and invisibly, who remains within the fold, and who will be cast out.

The sovereigns of the modern age, tech platforms, social feeds, protocol layers, do not break bones. They do not spill blood. They do not summon inquisitions in public squares. Instead, they break visibility. They sever reach. They erase presence. One day, you have a voice. A following. A platform. A sense of agency in the networked world. The next, you are silenced, not with a bang, but with a quiet removal, a link that no longer loads, a post that no longer appears, a shadow that no longer casts.

This is digital excommunication. It is not less severe than the old kind, it is in many ways more efficient, more scalable, more devastating. For in a world where reputation is capital, where attention is economy, and where visibility is survival, the removal of these things is not symbolic. It is existential. The subject is not merely muted, they are unpersoned. They are transformed from participant to ghost, stripped of the ability to contest, to protest, to be.

And yet, this is not an accident. It is design. These systems were not merely built to enable communication, they were also built to control it. Deplatforming, shadowbanning, account suspensions, algorithmic downranking, these are not glitches in the democratic ideal of the internet. They are feudal instruments of enforcement, mechanisms that reinforce the sovereign power of platforms through the quiet terror of erasure.

Loyalty today is maintained not through public trials, but through the fear of disappearance. No need to execute dissent when you can render it irrelevant. No need to argue with the heretic when the feed refuses to show his face. The populace learns quickly. They adjust. They modulate their speech. They choose their alignments carefully. They speak the right phrases, follow the right figures, avoid the wrong signals, not because they are convinced, but because they know the cost of transgression is not rebuke, but obliteration.

And so, let this chapter be understood not only as an analysis, but as a warning.

To the modern Prince: if you do not control the means of communication, you are not sovereign. Your voice, your story, your presence, these things exist at the mercy of platforms that are not your own. And should you stray too far from the acceptable script, should your influence begin to threaten the ordained architecture, you may find yourself cast into the void, your followers unable to find you, your ideas deranked into silence, your digital identity revoked like a heretic's blessing.

In earlier centuries, an exiled ruler could flee into the wilderness, rally new forces, return with arms. But in this new kingdom of glass and code, there is no wilderness left. Every terrain is owned. Every node is monitored. Every channel is bound to rules that you did not write.

If you are to survive, if you are to rule, you must do more than speak.

You must own the space in which your speech lives.

You must architect redundancy. You must build parallel infrastructure. You must weave your myth across domains that cannot all be erased at once.

For the architecture of digital banishment is real.

It is growing.

And those who ignore it will one day vanish, without a trace, and without a war.

The Mechanics of Modern Banishment

Digital excommunication wears many faces. Some are loud and final. Others are silent, imperceptible, and far more insidious. In this new regime of platform power, exile is not necessarily declared, it is executed. The sentence is not spoken aloud. It is written into the code, buried in the algorithm, whispered through shadowed protocols. And yet, the effect is absolute.

The most visible form is deplatforming, the outright deletion of an account, the revocation of access, the erasure of presence. One moment, a person exists within the public square. The next, they are gone. Their profile vanishes. Their posts are removed. Their history is wiped clean, as if they were never there. No parting message. No recourse. It is the digital equivalent of medieval exile: a casting out that renders the subject socially radioactive. Their followers scatter. Their collaborators go silent. Their name, once signal, becomes stigma. The memory of them begins to decay under the weight of silence. This is the cleanest and most brutal form of erasure, total and terminal.

But there is a quieter variant, one that strikes not through removal, but through invisibility. Shadowbanning. In this form of punishment, the subject is allowed to remain, but not to be seen. They can still speak, but their words disappear into the void. Their posts no longer appear in timelines. Their comments no longer notify others. Their names cease to surface in searches. And yet, to them, everything appears normal. This is not censorship through confrontation. It is censorship through silence, a psychological torture that simulates freedom while denying its substance. The victim continues to perform, unaware that their stage has been darkened, their audience dismissed. It is a kind of digital entombment, buried alive in the feed.

Another tactic is demonetization, a quieter, economic form of exile. Here, the individual is not silenced outright. They are still allowed to create, to share, to speak. But the mechanisms by which they earn are revoked. Ads are disabled. Sponsorships dry up. Payment rails are severed. Their content may still circulate, but the engine that turns attention into livelihood has been dismantled. This is a different kind of punishment, a forced descent into unpaid labor. A return to digital serfdom, where performance persists but the harvest is denied. It is not death, but devaluation.

Then there is the invisible hand of soft censorship, content downranked, visibility throttled, reach curtailed without warning or explanation. The individual has not broken any rules. No accusations have been made. No public announcement has been issued. And yet, the effect is unmistakable: posts that once spread widely now stagnate. Engagement plummets. Recommendations disappear. The algorithm no longer blesses the subject with presence. And because no clear cause is given, there is nothing to appeal, nothing to contest. The punishment exists in a fog, unacknowledged, unspoken, but unmistakable. This is power at its most refined: governance without declaration, discipline without accusation.

Finally, there is the broader ritual of blacklisting and boycott, a form of excommunication that extends beyond the borders of any single platform. Here, the punishment is social and economic, enforced by a decentralized swarm of institutions, collaborators, and former allies. The accused finds themselves locked out not just of speech, but of infrastructure: removed from mailing lists, cut off from sponsors, payment processors, and partnerships. They are quietly severed from the networks that made their presence possible. This is the modern equivalent of placing someone under interdict, no one may touch them, speak with them, or do business with them without risk of guilt by association. The execution is bloodless but devastating.

What unites all these forms is their absence of due process. There is no trial, no clear chain of events, no defined sentence. The punishment is delivered by private actors through private rules, often algorithmically enforced, and rarely explained. These are not acts of law. They are acts of protocol. No court of appeal exists. And yet, their impact is total, because in a world where presence is power, to remove that presence is to unmake the person.

This is the new discipline of the digital age. It is not centralized but networked. Not legal, but structural. Not declared but enacted. Power no longer needs to jail or kill. It needs only to disconnect.

And so, the modern sovereign must ask not only how to build power, but how to defend it from erasure. Because in this world, exile no longer requires force. Only silence. And silence, once engineered into the system, becomes harder to break than any chain.

Excommunication as Political Control

In the medieval world, ultimate authority did not reside solely with kings. Armies could conquer land, but they could not confer legitimacy. That power belonged to the Church, and at its apex, to the Pope. His might was not measured in soldiers, but in the ability to define the moral order. A king could not rule without divine sanction. A monarch without the Church's blessing was not simply controversial, he was illegitimate. And should a ruler defy the papacy, a single declaration, a papal bull of excommunication, could unravel his authority. To be cast out was to become spiritually tainted, politically isolated, and socially vulnerable. Emperors knelt barefoot in the snow, not from fear of violence, but from fear of exile from the order that gave their power meaning.

That dynamic has not disappeared. It has only changed form. Today, the bishops are not draped in robes, they wear hoodies, write code, and maintain platforms. It is not cathedrals they command, but clouds. And yet, they still hold the power to decide who belongs, and who does not. The new sacraments are accounts, payment credentials, content distribution, search visibility. The new heresies are violations of Terms of Service. And the new excommunications are algorithmic, silent, and instantaneous.

When YouTube deletes your channel, it is not just content that is lost, it is livelihood, visibility, identity. Years of work vanish with the click of a moderation trigger. When Twitter (or X) suspends your account, you are no longer part of the public conversation. Your voice is removed from the agora. Your network collapses. Your influence bleeds out. When PayPal freezes your funds, you are economically exiled. You cannot trade, tip, transact, or build. And when Google delists your site, your ideas are buried beneath digital earth, functionally nonexistent. They are not censored in the traditional sense, they are disappeared, unlinked from the structures of search and discovery that give ideas life in the networked world.

This is not the tyranny of a censor's red pen. It is something more total and more refined. It is compliance by infrastructure, a mode of governance that does not need to jail or silence you explicitly. It simply removes your access. In this regime, freedom of speech still technically exists. But it is speech shouted into a void. Speech without distribution. Expression without platform. And in a world saturated by information, that is equivalent to nonexistence.

What remains is not liberty, but conditional presence. You may speak, but only if your voice does not trigger the protocols of removal. You may earn, but only if your values align with the payment stack. You may be seen, but only if the feed favors you. The sovereign of a digital domain need not persecute you. He need only disconnect you. And once disconnected, your reality ceases to matter. In the new world, visibility is life. And silence, algorithmic, infrastructural, or reputational, is death.

This is the logic of digital feudalism. It is not enforced by knights. It is enforced by platforms. The new bannermen are developers. The new cardinals are moderators. And the new Pope is protocol, the silent, unaccountable force that can bless or erase with equal ease.

So let it be understood:

The battle is no longer over what may be said.

It is over what may be seen.

And to be unseen, in a world ruled by platforms, is to be unmade.

Cancel Culture as Distributed Inquisition

What was once the pronouncement of a Church is now the verdict of a networked swarm. The rituals have changed. The vestments have changed. But the logic remains eerily familiar. "Cancel culture," for all its supposed ties to justice or accountability, is rarely about true rehabilitation. It is not a sober process of ethical reckoning. It is a ritual of purification, a collective purge, a performance of moral hygiene enacted not through courts, but through crowds.

The process is formulaic. A transgression is identified, real, exaggerated, or entirely fabricated. It can be a decade-old comment, a clumsy phrase, a political opinion, or simply a refusal to recite the current orthodoxy. Screenshots are dug up like sacred relics. Old videos resurface as if pulled from beneath cathedral stones. A thread is written. A case is made, not to a judge, but to the feed. Quote tweets function as torches.

Comment sections turn into tribunals. The crowd does not wait for the defense. It demands blood.

The punishment is not legal. It does not involve arrest or imprisonment. It is far more efficient: it is erasure. Visibility is revoked. Sponsors pull away, terrified of guilt by association. Collaborators grow silent. Emails go unanswered. Revenue dries up. The subject is not just criticized, they are rendered morally unfit for participation in polite society. They become toxic, untouchable, a kind of social leper marked not by disease, but by disobedience to the invisible order of the feed.

This is not justice. It is excommunication by mob. And like the inquisitions of old, it is not bound by truth, consistency, or process. It is bound by spectacle and emotional consensus. The question is not whether a sin was truly committed, but whether enough people feel that it was. The swarm does not ask for clarity, it demands submission. And even that may not be enough. An apology is expected, then dissected, then rejected for lacking sincerity. Silence is punished. Protest is punished. Irony is punished. There is no stable exit strategy once the ritual begins.

This is a new kind of power. It is not centralized. It does not need approval from a sovereign. It emerges from the crowd like a storm, chaotic, unstable, and brutally effective. It is not legal authority. It is social weather. And it can sweep away reputations, platforms, careers, and even lives, often without anyone claiming responsibility.

A wise Prince does not ignore this phenomenon. He studies it. He learns how it moves, how it builds, how it escalates. He sees that the swarm does not only destroy, it can be channeled. Directed. Weaponized. A scandal can be triggered with the right signal, the right framing, the right moment. A rival can be marked, and the mob summoned like fire. Just as medieval kings sometimes whispered in the ears of bishops, today's rulers whisper into timelines. They do not issue the sentence. They merely provide the kindling.

This is not a condemnation of the crowd. The crowd is not evil, it is primordial. It is the natural expression of outrage in a system with no courts and no crown. But the Prince must recognize that this outrage is not moral clarity, it is raw energy, and it is often indifferent to truth. That makes it dangerous. But it also makes it useful.

He who masters the spectacle does not fear cancellation.

He orchestrates it.

And in doing so, he learns what the Church once knew:

That to declare someone unfit is to shape the boundaries of the sacred.

The crowd does not need to be silenced. It needs to be led.

And the sovereign who understands this will not be its victim.

He will be its choir director.

The Power to Unperson

To unperson someone is not to kill them, it is to erase their social identity. It is not the destruction of a body, but the deletion of a name. The individual continues to exist in the physical world. They breathe, they move, they speak. But within the digital and social fabric, where visibility, access, and narrative determine existence, they have been removed. The record is gone. The context collapses. What remains is a shell, present in flesh but absent from meaning. They become, effectively, unreal.

The concept originates with George Orwell's 1984, where to be unpersoned was to vanish entirely from history, as if one had never existed. In that imagined dystopia, totalitarian control could reach backward in time, removing not just the living body, but the idea of the person. What Orwell envisioned as a terrifying fiction is now an automated function of modern life. It no longer requires the machinery of a state. It is performed by algorithms, platforms, and the invisible consensus of a crowd moving in digital unison. What once required clerics and decrees now requires only silence and code.

The process unfolds quietly. There is rarely a single, definitive moment. First, your name begins to slip from search results. Your account remains online, but increasingly difficult to find. Past posts disappear from timelines. Discovery engines delist your content. You are not deleted, exactly, you are obscured, faded out like an old photo. In some cases, your likeness is scrubbed from AI training sets, ensuring that you cannot be seen even in the hallucinations of future machines. Your Wikipedia entry, once a sign of cultural relevance, is vandalized or locked. Your website flagged as unsafe. Your username, lost or reassigned, becomes a placeholder for someone else. The sum of your digital identity begins to disintegrate.

As the deletion deepens, so too does the distance others keep. Followers are warned away, some by explicit notices, others by subtle signals. Accusations may circulate. Messages may go undelivered. Your name may no longer autocomplete. Your content no longer appears in feeds. Even those who once championed you hesitate. The casual retweet becomes risky. A simple like feels rebellious. Mentioning your name starts to feel like a breach of decorum. Unpersoning operates not just by removing you from view, it contaminates your proximity. Those near you shrink away, not because they believe the charges, but because they know the cost of association.

This is how the network kills. Not with sword or executioner, but with silence.

Your voice echoes, but there is no one there to hear it.

Your name still exists, but it is no longer called.

Your past remains, but its connections are severed.

You are not remembered as wrong. You are remembered as gone.

What is occurring is not mere censorship. It is something deeper and more final. It is symbolic execution, not the removal of liberty, but of relevance. The severing not of speech, but of social immortality. It is the conversion of a person into a cautionary tale. And in the age of platforms, that tale spreads faster than truth.

Unpersoning functions not only as punishment. It functions as message. It is discipline performed in public, even when it looks like absence. The Prince must understand this. To cast someone out from the digital commons is not just to remove a threat. It is to tell the entire network: this is what happens to those who disobey. The act is rarely acknowledged, but everyone understands it. It is the ritual of power made sterile and silent.

And it works.

People learn. They adapt. They internalize the lesson. They shift their speech, their posture, their tone. They grow cautious with words, selective with retweets, evasive in their allegiances. They do not need to be told where the line is, they infer it from the growing list of those who have vanished.

This is how modern power enforces itself, not through direct commands, but through the erasure of deviation so complete that resistance ceases to be imagined.

Thus, the sovereign does not merely fear unpersoning, he studies it. He learns its tempo, its signs, its triggers. And when necessary, he may even deploy it, not out of rage, but with calculation. Not to punish, but to demonstrate.

Because in the digital realm, death is no longer the ultimate punishment.

To be forgotten is.

Rituals of Purification

Just as medieval excommunication was not a mere administrative act but a ritualized spectacle, so too does modern digital erasure follow a precise and recognizable choreography. In the old world, the Church's declaration of excommunication was accompanied by ceremony, bells were rung, cloaks were torn, names were read aloud in trembling Latin. It was not enough to cut someone off from the sacred order; they had to be marked. They had to be seen as fallen.

Today, this process plays out not in cathedrals, but across timelines, quote tweets, and comment sections. And yet, the architecture is the same. It begins with a spark, often small, almost trivial. A tweet resurfaces. A video clip is clipped again. A comment is pulled out of context, isolated from its meaning but saturated with new emotional charge. This is the accusation, the moment the subject is brought to the attention of the modern tribunal. The tone is not inquiry, it is certainty. The transgression has already been decided. Now it must be witnessed.

What follows is reaction, the rapid, viral escalation of attention. Screenshots are taken. Threads are spun. Influencers, commentators, and spectators begin to weigh in. Some offer outrage, others disappointment. Many simply join the chorus, sensing blood in the water. Visibility explodes, not in celebration, but in condemnation. Every new voice adds weight. Every share tightens the noose. At this point, the subject has become a character, and the character has become a symbol. Nuance vanishes. The audience demands only one thing: a reckoning.

Soon, the demand emerges. Apologize. Recant. Step away. Be silent. There is rarely a formal arbiter. The command is issued not from a throne but from the feed itself. It comes through tone, consensus, expectation. If the accused responds too quickly, they are called insincere. If they wait, they are accused of arrogance. If they deny, they are declared beyond redemption. The only acceptable script is repentance, but even then, it may be too late. Because the ritual is not designed for redemption. It is designed for removal.

Then comes the fall. Removal is rarely executed by a single hand. Sponsors cut ties. Platforms begin to suspend, demonetize, or delete. Videos disappear. Articles are taken down. Access is revoked. Infrastructure evaporates. What once took years to build, an audience, a reputation, a livelihood, is dismantled in hours. But the most haunting moment is what follows: the aftermath. Friends go silent. Collaborators withdraw. Those who remain in proximity face their own test: denounce or be tainted. Guilt by association is not a metaphor, it is an algorithmic contagion. To stand too close to the unclean is to risk becoming unclean yourself.

This entire sequence is not random. It is ritual theater with real teeth. It is not just social, it is economic, reputational, existential. It does not merely seek to punish behavior. It seeks to redefine a person's place in the moral order. What makes it so potent, so unchallengeable, is that it requires no central authority. There is no judge. No jury. No Church. The mob enforces the code, and the platforms, sensing volatility, follow the noise. Moderators don't lead the hunt. They arrive after the fire has already been lit, and they simply extinguish the remains.

This is the machinery of cultural enforcement in the networked age. It is leaderless, decentralized, and yet terrifyingly coordinated. And it is precisely this structure that gives it power.

A Prince who ignores these rituals does so at his peril. To pretend they are not real, or that they will not touch him, is to misunderstand the landscape of power. For in the age of platforms, power flows through spectacle, and spectacle is governed by ritual. The wise sovereign does not simply watch the mob, he listens to it, studies its rhythms, learns how it breathes.

And if he is clever, he learns not only how to survive it, but how to wield it, against rivals who grow too bold, allies who stray too far, or narratives that threaten the coherence of his realm. To understand the ritual is to understand the new theater of control.

Because in this world, the altar may be digital, but the sacrifices are real.

Surveillance and Preemptive Obedience

The power of excommunication in the digital age does not rely solely on its execution. Its true force lies in its anticipation. What gives the threat its potency is not how often it is carried out, but how constantly it looms. And that threat is made exponentially more effective by the reality, or even just the perception, of omnipresent surveillance.

In a world where every post is tracked, every message archived, every interaction measured and scored, individuals begin to moderate themselves. They soften their jokes. They delete old tweets. They avoid speaking on certain topics. They learn, gradually and instinctively, which words to avoid, which opinions to mute, which tones to adopt in order to signal alignment with the dominant current. What results is not simply a compliant population, it is a self-censoring one. And self-censorship is the most efficient form of control.

This is the logic of the panopticon, a concept first imagined in the 18th century: a prison designed so that the inmates never know when they are being watched and thus behave as though they always are. No guard needs to patrol every cell. No command needs to be given. The architecture itself does the work. The possibility of observation becomes its own form of discipline. And so, even when the algorithm is not actively punishing, banning, suppressing, or removing, its presence, or the fear of its presence, is enough to enforce behavioral conformity.

The subject may never be told what not to say. But they learn, through the erasure of others, the signals of danger. They witness the sudden vanishing of accounts, the public implosions, the scandals, the quiet disappearances. They see what happens to those who speak too loudly, too early, too freely. And so they choose the safer path. They comply, not because they were told to, but because they imagine the consequences.

This is power at its most refined: power that does not need to announce itself. The ruler does not lift a finger. The sovereign platform does not issue a decree. The algorithm does not need to act. The mere expectation of action achieves the result. This is not brute force. It is a form of governance that operates without visible governance. A power that maintains order through ambient fear.

And in this structure, obedience is preemptive. Compliance becomes second nature. The people do not wait to be punished, they discipline themselves to avoid the possibility. Thought itself begins to bend. Not through violence. Not through law. But through design, repetition, and the silent pressure of the feed.

It is, in many ways, the dream of every ruler since time began: a society where the population regulates its own behavior, not out of conviction, but out of fear of exclusion. Not because they believe in the system, but because they know what lies outside it is worse.

They do not fight the system. They do not challenge it.

They remain inside it, quiet, careful, curated.

Because to step outside is to risk being unpersoned.

And in the modern age, there is no wilderness left in which to hide.

The Weaponization of Platforms

Digital platforms claim neutrality. It is their default posture, their shield, their defense. They present themselves as open commons, passive infrastructures, impartial arenas in which ideas are merely exchanged, content is merely hosted, and users are merely served. But this posture is a fiction. No platform is truly neutral. None can be. Every digital environment is shaped by policies, informed by priorities, and inevitably embedded with politics. What can be said, what is promoted, what is punished, all of this is curated, structured, and enforced according to values, incentives, and pressures that exist far beneath the surface.

Moderation, the mechanism that claims to uphold safety and order, is not simply a set of tools. It is an instrument of power. It is not neutral code, it is a method of governance, often opaque, always consequential. The moderation team is not a passive force. It is the court, the police, the priesthood, and the judge, all rolled into one. It determines what is allowed to exist. And in a networked society, to decide what exists is to decide what is real.

The savvy understand this. And so, they act accordingly. A well-timed campaign, carried out by an ideological faction or a vested interest group, can pressure a platform into removing or banning a rival voice. The campaign does not need to prove harm. It only needs to generate enough noise. Controversy is manufactured, outrage is simulated, and the platform, eager to avoid disruption or bad press, responds by erasing the target. The public sees a moderation decision. But in truth, they are witnessing a successful political maneuver disguised as protocol enforcement.

The same tactic can be seen in coordinated flagging operations. A group, acting in concert, floods a content moderation system with reports, exploiting the automation of enforcement. The goal is not to contest the idea in public, it is to silence it in private. The platform's response may be justified as algorithmic, procedural, or compliant with policy. But underneath it is a deliberate suppression, carried out not by debate, but by exploiting the mechanisms of control.

And then there is the third layer, perhaps the most powerful of all: economic coercion. Platforms do not answer only to users. They answer to advertisers. A controversy, real or invented, can trigger a panic among brands. Headlines swirl. Pressure mounts. Revenue is threatened. And when the business model is at risk, platforms act swiftly. They do not remove content because it is false or dangerous. They remove it because its presence has become expensive. This is not about truth. It is about cost.

These are not accidents. They are not bugs in the system. They are features of the new political landscape, standard weapons in what we can now call techno-feudal warfare. Just as medieval lords fought through proxies, assassins, and bribes, modern sovereigns battle through deplatforming, demonetization, and narrative framing. Platforms are the battlegrounds. Moderation systems are the weapons. And users are the foot soldiers, often unaware of the game they're playing.

The modern Prince must not be naïve. He must never take a platform's neutrality at face value. He must see clearly: every feed has a filter, every protocol has a preference, every rule is a gate. And behind that gate stands someone with an interest in who enters, who speaks, and who disappears.

To rule effectively in this age, a Prince must not only master the art of messaging or myth-making. He must learn to operate within the terrain of platform warfare. He must understand how noise becomes policy. How outrage becomes censorship. How market pressure becomes exile. And he must be prepared, not just to defend against these tactics, but to use them when necessary.

Because in the realm of platforms, power does not shout.

It whispers through moderation queues, recommendation engines, and terms of service.

And the sovereign who ignores this terrain will not be overthrown.

He will be removed, silently, with a click.

No trial. No rebellion.

Just another line of code,

marking the end of his reign.

IX

The Infinite Court

Parasocial Rule, Fandom Allegiance, and the Performance of Power in the Feudal Feed. Every Prince lives in a court. This has always been true. Power, by its nature, requires proximity, an audience, a stage, a place where rule is enacted and observed. In centuries past, this court was a physical space. It was carved from stone and wood, lit by torches, guarded by knights. It had structure: thrones, councils, processions, chambers of decision. The sovereign sat at its center, seen by all, shielded by ritual and hierarchy. Access was limited. Appearances were rare. Authority was measured in distance and control.

But the court has changed. It has not vanished, it has migrated. Today, the Prince's court is no longer bound by geography or walls. It is made not of marble, but of glass, pixels, timelines, and comment sections. It is a place that cannot be touched, only seen. It is not a single room, but an endless stream. The court of the modern sovereign is infinite: always open, always shifting, always hungry. It never sleeps. It never forgets. And it is filled not just with subjects, but with strangers, critics, competitors, and ghosts.

This is the new theater of power. Here, the sovereign does not sit above the people. He flows among them, in feeds, in posts, in livestreams and updates. He no longer issues decrees in gilded halls. He speaks into the algorithm, casting signals into the current, hoping they will land, be amplified, be seen. His words must fight for space in a sea of noise. His face must compete with a thousand others. And always, always, he must perform.

There is no privacy in this court. There is no backstage. The Prince is always watched, not only by his enemies, but by his allies, his followers, his rivals, and the indifferent crowd that waits to be entertained. His life becomes his language. Every gesture is content. Every silence is interpreted. Every moment is political. The sovereign is no longer remote. He is hyper-visible. But this visibility does not grant security. It demands exposure. And exposure, in this world, is risk.

He is never alone. He is never unobserved. And yet, paradoxically, he must remain untouchable. He must appear accessible, but never ordinary. He must be mythic, but never robotic. He must live among his people but never be fully one of them. This is the paradox of digital rule: to survive, the sovereign must be a presence, a projection, a symbol that anyone can see themselves in, yet no one can fully grasp. He must be both mirror and mask.

This is not a failure of sovereignty. It is its evolution. Power has not disappeared. It has been reformatted. In this world, the old pillars of rule, law, land, lineage, have been replaced by visibility, charisma, and narrative control. To rule now is to be seen, shared, and believed. To be ignored is to become irrelevant. To be misperceived is to be dethroned.

And so, the Prince must understand the mechanics of this infinite court. He must know that loyalty is now parasocial, a fragile intimacy formed through screens, dependent on attention and illusion. He must grasp that obedience is now emotional, shaped by aesthetic, tone, and timing. He must accept that authenticity is manufactured, not faked, but constructed, layer by layer, through performance.

Enemies in this court do not strike with armies. They strike with memes, with clips, with threads designed to stain. Friends, once loyal, may betray him not with daggers but with silence, the deadliest weapon in a world of constant affirmation. And the crowd? The crowd that once lifted him high will one day turn. Not because he failed, but because he changed, or stood still, or became uninteresting.

To survive in the infinite court, a Prince must become more than clever. He must become mythic, but human. Present enough to be loved. Distant enough to be revered. He must learn to reflect the desires of the crowd without being consumed by them. He must become a mirror that shows everyone a version of themselves but reveals nothing of himself. A sovereign not of land, but of attention. A ruler not of subjects, but of symbols.

This is the burden of the new throne. It offers no crown, only exposure. No citadel, only stream. But it offers something greater than territory: timeless presence. And in this age, to rule is not to command. It is to be unforgettable.

Court by Feed, Not by Blood

In the old world, the court was a fixed and sacred place. It was a physical location, anchored in stone and tradition, where power was both enacted and symbolized. Loyalty was earned through proximity, gestures, and time spent in the ruler's presence. To ascend within the court was to be seen in the right hall, at the right hour, wearing the right colors, saying the right things. Authority was not only spoken; it was staged, through hierarchy, ceremony, and architecture. To approach the sovereign required passage through corridors of formality and layers of protocol. Distance signified importance. Access was earned, measured, and rare.

Today, that geography has collapsed. The court has migrated to the feed. It exists nowhere and everywhere, fluid, ephemeral, and always awake. There are no gates. No guards. No official threshold. One does not pass through marble columns or bow before heralds. One simply swipes. A single motion of the thumb is enough to enter the digital presence of the sovereign. And just as quickly, one can leave.

This accessibility is unprecedented. The modern sovereign is more visible than any king in history. His words arrive not in proclamations carved into stone or delivered from balconies, but in livestreams, tweets, and vertical videos. His moods are interpreted through emojis. His policies are measured by replies. His alliances are tracked in follows and unfollows. Every action, every like, every retweet, every reply, is now a performance in the court of public perception. And the audience is vast, global, and instant. There is no private chamber where the ruler can think quietly. There is no shadow in which he can prepare his next move.

This transformation has created a paradox: the sovereign is now always available, yet increasingly vulnerable. He is both idol and spectacle. He may hold the attention of millions, but he must constantly earn it. There is no retreat behind castle walls, no velvet rope separating ruler from ruled. The crowd demands his presence, not as a rare symbol of national strength, but as a daily participant in their scrolling lives. They expect content. They expect updates. They expect vulnerability, engagement, spontaneity. The ruler must not only be wise or powerful. He must also be relatable, emotionally attuned, capable of being liked and shared and saved.

The digital court has no doors. No curfews. No guards to close the gate. It is always open, always moving, always watching. The Prince does not rule from a throne of oak and iron, but from a stream of flickering content. He is judged not by legacy, but by visibility. And the feed is a cruel throne, welcoming, demanding, and infinitely hungry.

To survive this condition, the Prince must learn the art of ruling through performance. Not mere showmanship, but the careful choreography of authenticity, presence, and distance. He must know how to be seen without being consumed, how to reveal without being hollowed out. He must master the balance between presence and mystique, between accessibility and sovereignty. He must learn to shape his image across endless exposure, without allowing that image to be shattered by overexposure.

For in this age, to rule is not to command from afar, it is to dwell in the court of everyone's attention. To be available without being reduced. To be watched without becoming ordinary. The Prince is no longer shielded by ceremony. He is surrounded by commentary. And his reign will not be measured by the gold in his vaults, but by the power of his presence in the feed.

In such a world, the challenge is not merely to appear powerful.

It is to remain sovereign in the spotlight,

without letting the spotlight burn you down.

The Parasocial Crown

In a traditional monarchy, the people knew their ruler's name, but rarely his face. The sovereign was a distant figure, abstract, symbolic, elevated above the mundane realities of daily life. His likeness might appear on coins, stamped in metal to signify both currency and kingship. Stories about him would pass through taverns and marketplaces, distorted by myth and rumor, but his person remained cloaked in ritual and distance. He was revered not because he was familiar, but precisely because he was unfamiliar. Mystery was part of the throne's architecture.

Today, that veil has been lifted. Or at least, it appears to have been. The modern sovereign, whether a political leader, cultural figure, entrepreneur, or content monarch, is no longer a remote figure glimpsed through ceremony. He is seen constantly. Heard daily. Swiped past hourly. The digital subject does not encounter the sovereign through formal channels, but through feeds, reels, livestreams, and behind-the-scenes videos. The sovereign shares thoughts. Shows his morning routine. Makes jokes. Cries. Posts. Replies. The result is not merely visibility, it is the illusion of intimacy.

This illusion is what we now call parasocial connection: the one-sided relationship in which a follower feels deeply bonded to a public figure who does not know they exist. The follower feels understood. Seen. Cared for. They feel not just inspired but known. And from this illusion of mutuality grows a powerful emotion and loyalty. But it is not the loyalty of the subject to a distant king. It is the loyalty of the fan to someone they believe is their friend. Their mentor. Their secret mirror.

Parasociality transforms passive spectators into active participants. The subject does not merely admire the sovereign, they defend him. They fight his battles in comment sections. They evangelize his message across platforms. They correct misquotes, denounce rivals, echo his language, and wear his style like a uniform. In this form, fandom becomes fealty. And it is this dynamic, this voluntary, enthusiastic, unpaid army, that gives the modern Prince a new kind of power: not one built on fear or lineage, but on emotional intimacy at scale.

But such power comes with profound danger.

Because in a parasocial relationship, loyalty is not governed by reason or tradition. It is governed by expectation, and expectations, when unspoken, are impossible to satisfy. The follower does not simply want content. They want confirmation. They want to feel chosen, special, spiritually aligned. They believe they are owed not just access, but purity, an unbroken alignment between the sovereign's persona and the follower's projection. And when that alignment breaks, when the Prince is caught in hypocrisy, when he makes a mistake, when he fails to live up to the intimacy the follower imagined, loyalty curdles into betrayal.

The parasocial subject does not walk away quietly. They feel deceived. Personally wounded. And so, they do not retreat, they retaliate. They turn from acolytes to inquisitors. The very intimacy that once sustained the relationship now becomes the weapon. They know the sovereign's habits, his voice, his contradictions. They use the tools he gave them to burn the throne they once bowed to.

This is the risk of ruling by intimacy: when the myth breaks, it shatters like glass.

Thus, the modern Prince must learn to master parasocial dynamics. He must understand that visibility is not the same as vulnerability. He must know that giving everything is not the same as giving meaningfully. He must offer glimpses of closeness, stories, struggles, laughter, humanity, but never collapse into ordinariness. The subject must feel near him, but never equal to him. There must always remain a sliver of mystery, a veil that cannot be pierced, a sacred distance in the midst of endless proximity.

He must allow the audience to feel close, but not to claim him. He must be relatable, but not replaceable. Human, but mythic. Seen, but not possessed. For in this new age, power does not reside in titles or territory. It resides in the emotions of millions. And the sovereign who forgets that love is not the same as loyalty will find his court filled not with followers, but with former believers sharpening their knives.

Sovereignty as Spectacle

Machiavelli once said it is better for a ruler to be feared than loved. But that was in an era where power was enforced through armies, borders, and the constant threat of violence. In the age of the infinite court, that equation has shifted. Today, it is no longer better to be feared than loved. It is better to be watched. Visibility is the new engine of power. Sovereignty is no longer maintained through force; it is sustained through attention.

The modern Prince does not need a military to preserve his rule. He does not need fortresses, nor fleets, nor the traditional symbols of command. What he needs is an audience. Because in the digital realm, to be watched is to exist. Attention confers presence. Visibility confers legitimacy. If the people are watching, the Prince lives. If they are not, he is dying in silence. The algorithm will not save him. The feed will forget him. The court will move on.

This is the reality of spectacle as sovereignty. Power must now be performed in real time. A stream, a post, a story, a tweet, each is not just content, but a proclamation of rule. The sovereign's daily rituals are no longer cloaked in mystery, they are narrated, filtered, captioned, shared. Each post is a signal: I am here. I am relevant. I am worthy of your gaze. And each comment beneath it, each reply or reaction, becomes the modern version of palace gossip, court intrigue, or whispered alliances.

The court speaks, not in letters or declarations, but in likes, shares, and quote tweets.

But this attention is fragile. The court of the feed is fickle, volatile, always one swipe away from disinterest. The Prince must remain fascinating. He cannot rely on legacy, only on momentum. His myth must be in constant motion. He must narrate himself endlessly, framing his journey, justifying his failures, amplifying his victories. He must become not just a ruler, but a drama. A living story. A character whose presence generates gravity. A ritual unfolding in public, one post at a time.

And this performance cannot stop. There are no intermissions in the infinite court. No time to withdraw, reflect, or disappear. If the sovereign becomes boring, uncertain, or too opaque, the people do not revolt, they scroll. They leave quietly, without rebellion. Their attention flows elsewhere. A new face appears. A fresher myth. A stronger signal. And just like that, the old sovereign is replaced. Not by decree. Not by vote. But by neglect.

To rule in this age is to understand that power flows not through coercion, but through captivation. The gaze of the people is both crown and noose. The Prince must wear it lightly, but never let it slip. For the moment he is no longer watched, he no longer rules. And the feed, relentless and bottomless, will carry on without him, as if he were never there at all.

The Fragility of Favor

In a medieval court, losing the king's favor was dangerous. It could mean exile, disgrace, or even death. Favor was personal, finite, and tightly held, bestowed by a singular sovereign whose gaze conferred status, whose silence could destroy it. But in the infinite court of today, the danger flows in the opposite direction. It is not the monarch's favor that determines survival, it is the favor of the audience. And to lose that is not merely dangerous. It is fatal.

The digital crowd is a force unlike any previous courtly assembly. It is vast, unstable, and emotionally volatile. Its loyalty is always conditional. Its expectations are shapeshifting. Its moods do not shift with seasons or reason, but with algorithmic amplification, waves of outrage, ecstasy, and fatigue pulsing across the network with no warning and no accountability. The audience is both sovereign and mob, army and executioner. They build you up only to test how fast they can take you down.

It takes very little for the crowd to turn. One poorly timed opinion, a "bad take," as they call it, can spark a revolt. One leaked message, pulled out of context and magnified by the feed, can cause followers to vanish overnight. And sometimes, the danger lies in saying nothing at all. Silence in the face of controversy, ambiguity during a crisis, even a perceived delay in performance can trigger suspicion, then anger, then abandonment. There is no due process in this court. No inquiry, no deliberation. The crowd moves like a storm, fast, chaotic, and often against those it once adored.

Worse still, the sovereign is often punished not for who he is, but for who the audience imagined him to be. The betrayal is not always real, it is projected. A myth is broken, and the crowd responds not with disappointment, but with vengeance. The Prince is not judged fairly; he is judged emotionally, collectively, and often irrationally. This is the reality of modern rule: you are punished not for breaking promises, but for failing to embody a fantasy.

A wise Prince must never become dependent on affection. Affection is sweet, but it is fleeting. He must resist the temptation to mistake applause for permanence. He must understand that favor is not a throne to sit on, it is a current. It flows, it changes, it betrays. And so, he must learn the deeper art of cyclical survival: how to rise with momentum, how to disappear with grace, how to return with myth renewed. He must learn when to be seen and when to vanish. When to speak, and when to let the storm pass without him.

Favor is not a possession. It is a pattern. A rhythm. A tide. The Prince does not stop the tide. He does not beg for its return. He rides it while it carries him, and when it recedes, he lets it go, knowing it will rise again. For in the infinite court, no favor lasts forever. But for those who master its flow, neither does exile.

The Performance of Authenticity

The infinite court does not merely demand presence, it demands authenticity. The sovereign is no longer permitted to remain aloof behind layers of symbolism and ritual. He must appear as a person, not just a persona. The crowd wants to see his flaws, his doubts, his private moments. They crave transparency, but only the kind that flatters their expectations. And so, authenticity itself becomes a performance, a carefully orchestrated illusion of openness that walks a razor-thin line between honesty and control.

Too little vulnerability, and the sovereign is accused of being distant, artificial, or out of touch. Too much, and he is branded weak, unstable, or unworthy of reverence. He must present himself as vulnerable, but never pathetic. As relatable, but never ordinary. As honest, but never controversial. As funny, but never foolish. Each quality must be filtered through precision, crafted to appear spontaneous, while serving a larger narrative of legitimacy and connection.

This is not deception. It is curation. Strategic selfhood. In the infinite court, where every post is a performance and every reaction is public, the sovereign must master the art of expressing truth without surrendering control. Authenticity, to be effective, must be timed, shaped, and framed. A story of personal failure, delivered with the right tone, can become a badge of strength, a symbol of resilience rather than weakness. A confession, made at the right moment, can become a ritual of loyalty, an opportunity for the crowd to forgive, to rally, to reattach themselves to the myth. Even a glimpse into "real life", a messy room, a tired face, an unscripted moment, can function not as a break in the performance, but as a myth-building event, reinforcing the idea that the sovereign is "just like us," even if he is not.

But this balancing act must be dynamic. The sovereign must be curated, yes, but never mechanical. Predictability is death in the court of infinite attention. The feed devours routine. If the Prince becomes too expected, he becomes background noise. Yet the opposite is no safer. Too much unpredictability, too much chaos, and the people begin to fear him. They retreat from instability. They want to feel like they know him, but they must never feel like they've figured him out completely.

This is the secret of controlled vulnerability. It is not about exposure, but about the illusion of access, the feeling that the sovereign has opened the gates to his inner self, even as his true core remains protected, unseen, intact. The Prince must be skilled in revealing just enough to bond, but never so much that he dissolves the myth. He must allow the crowd to believe they understand him, while always retaining a part of himself they can never touch. Because the moment the mystery disappears, the magic dies. And without magic, no sovereign survives the spotlight for long.

In the age of the infinite court, the sovereign does not just rule by attention. He rules by narrated intimacy. And his greatest weapon is the story he tells, about himself.

Court Jesters, Courtiers, and Rivals

In every court, there are recognizable archetypes, timeless roles that appear again and again, regardless of era or empire. There are the jesters, who appear to entertain, but speak truths too dangerous to come from the mouth of the sovereign himself. Their jokes carry blades. There are the courtiers, those who flatter, gossip, and maneuver, always presenting a mask of loyalty while angling for advantage behind closed doors. And there are the rivals, those who imitate the Prince with just enough difference to remain under the radar, waiting, watching, ready to move when he falters.

The infinite court has not erased these roles, it has multiplied them. The jester now appears as the irreverent influencer, the comedic voice who "just asks questions" but plants seeds of doubt. The courtier is the collaborator who basks in proximity to power, mining clout from every association, while slowly building a brand of their own. The rival is often born from within: a follower once loyal, now exiled, who uses the Prince's own techniques, his tone, his memes, his aesthetic, against him. And because the court is visible, endless, and performative, these roles are not confined to private chambers. They are played out in public, in real time, in the scrollable theater of timelines and feeds.

A Prince who does not recognize this is not a ruler, he is a placeholder. The infinite court is not merely a stage for governance. It is a breeding ground for coups. A meme that amuses today may be the first brick in the wall of your downfall. It begins with laughter, spreads through irony, and ends in detachment. A thread that sings your praises might not be admiration, it might be strategic positioning, laying the groundwork for your replacement. And the platform itself, once your kingdom, may begin to starve your reach, reroute your audience, and silently prepare your successor. There is no ceremony to dethronement in the infinite court. One day the feed simply moves on.

The Prince must live with this awareness. He is not just governing; he is constantly defending the symbolic crown. The smile must hide the watchful eye. A smart sovereign learns to reward loyalty but never becomes dependent on it. He elevates new voices, but never lets them rise too quickly, lest they believe they can do without him. He listens to jesters, because in their satire lies insight, but he never lets their mockery define the narrative.

Most importantly, he understands that not all followers are equal. He cultivates layers within the court. The outer circle is noisy, full of praise, critique, demand, and performance. It is where spectacles thrive, but where betrayal is born. The inner circle is quieter, those who do not compete for attention, but who offer counsel, stability, and deep allegiance. The true sovereign does not rule from the spotlight. He rules from the center, invisible to most, yet essential to all. His power lies not in how many see him, but in how many depend on his presence, whether they realize it or not.

And the court, as always, must be fed. It hungers for content. It craves entertainment. It demands narrative, drama, vulnerability, and myth. The banquet never ends. The clout feast continues. The Prince may be king, but only as long as he knows that every gesture is a performance, and every performance is a test.

In the age of the infinite court, ruling is surviving.

And surviving means knowing that the crown is never fully yours, it is on loan from the crowd.

Banquets of Content, Feasts of Clout

The court must be fed. In the medieval world, banquets were acts of politics as much as celebration, feasts that affirmed status, displayed wealth, and bound subjects to the sovereign through the performance of abundance. In the digital realm, the feast is content. The modern Prince does not offer bread or wine. He offers threads, reels, reflections, takes. These are the dishes set daily before the court. The audience arrives hungry, insatiable, expectant, and they demand to be served.

But what they consume is not nourishment. It is attention disguised as sustenance. The likes, the shares, the applause, they seem like tributes. They appear as signs of loyalty, of love, of favor. But in truth, they are expressions of need. The more you feed the court, the more it craves. No amount of content can satisfy the algorithm's appetite or the crowd's emotional void. The sovereign who mistakes this constant hunger for affection risks becoming not a ruler, but a servant, enslaved to performance, producing endlessly just to stay visible.

This is the great trap of the infinite court: the illusion that visibility equals authority. That to rule is to appear. That to be off-screen is to be forgotten. The Prince must resist this pull. He must remember that power lies not in the frequency of presence, but in the quality of command. The sovereign must master the timing of ritual, to post with intent, not desperation; to speak when silence would speak louder; to withdraw not out of fear, but to heighten return. Disappearance, when strategic, is not absence, it is mystique.

When the Prince does feed his court, the meal must be more than calories. It must be symbolic: every post should reaffirm his myth, each image or sentence another brushstroke in the portrait of the legend he is constructing. It must be thematic: not noise, but signal, a message that deepens the bond between ruler and subject, that says not just "I am here," but "we are bound." It must feel exclusive, as if those who see it have been granted rare access to the sovereign's inner chamber. And it must be relational, offering not just information or entertainment, but the feeling of personal connection. A single reply from the Prince can become a sacred relic in the hands of a follower.

The sovereign who understands this builds more than a following, he builds a court that defends him in his absence, that upholds his myth when he is silent, that spreads his gospel even when he sleeps. But the sovereign who overfeeds, who posts for approval, who reacts instead of leads, who tries to meet every demand, will find that constant giving breeds dependence, fatigue, and eventual resentment. The court turns. Not because it is hungry, but because it has been fed too often without meaning.

To rule well is to feed wisely. To post with purpose. To vanish with power. To make each message not a snack, but a sacrament. That is the feast the court remembers. And that is how the Prince endures.

X

The Mirror and The Mask

In the final days of his life, Niccolò Machiavelli, stripped of title and influence, wandered the hills outside Florence, exiled from the court he once advised. Though dismissed by power, he was not undone by it. Each evening, he returned to his modest estate, shed the dust of the countryside, donned the robes of his lost station, and sat alone at his desk. There, by candlelight, he communed not with courtiers, but with ghosts. He opened the works of Livy, Tacitus, and Caesar, and he spoke to them not as a student, but as an equal. "For four hours," he wrote in a letter to a friend, "I feel no boredom, I forget every worry, I do not fear poverty or death."

In this ritual, Machiavelli was not pretending. He was remembering. He was recovering the architecture of power, built not of castles or gold, but of thought. And it was in exile, not in favor, that he composed his most enduring work: The Prince.

Today, the world Machiavelli knew has collapsed. Power no longer resides in thrones or parliaments. It flows through platforms, timelines, dashboards, and protocols. Yet the essential lessons he gave us remain. The names have changed. The tools have changed. The battlefield has changed. But the game? The game endures.

You, the modern Prince, do not rule a city-state. You govern attention. You are not crowned with laurel, but with metrics. You are judged not by legacy, but by engagement. Your kingdom is borderless. Your court is infinite. And every moment you are watched, weighed, and whisperingly betrayed by those who smile at your feed.

In this world, sovereignty is no longer fixed. It is elastic, borrowed, and performative. You do not own it, you maintain it, moment by moment, post by post. The people do not fear you. They do not even truly know you. But they consume you. And in that consumption lies both your power and your peril.

Machiavelli understood this duality. In his time, the Prince needed to appear virtuous while acting with cunning. He needed to be lion and fox, adored and feared. Today, you must appear authentic while remaining mythic. You must be vulnerable, but invulnerable. Present, but unreachable. You must become a mirror that reflects everyone's desire, and a mask that no one can fully remove.

Your court does not convene in marble halls. It scrolls. It likes. It lurks. It judges without speaking. It crowns without warning. It destroys without remorse. One day you are their icon. The next, their shame. A misstep becomes a meme. A silence becomes a scandal. A joke becomes a trial.

And yet, this is not a warning. It is an invitation.

To rule in the age of the infinite court is to accept the performance as the throne itself. You must become fluent in symbolism, economy, aesthetics, and story. Every feed is a battlefield. Every comment is a cipher. Every message is a maneuver. There are no neutral posts. Every utterance either builds your sovereignty or undermines it. To be seen is to be claimed. To be misunderstood is to be rewritten.

You must not seek to control the court. You must learn to dance with it. Let others obsess over rules and platforms. You will build rituals. You will mint tokens of trust, artifacts of meaning. You will give your followers not just content, but identity. Because those who see themselves in your story will defend you as they would their own reflection.

The true sovereign in this age does not govern through force or decree. He governs through narrative gravity. He is not the loudest voice, but the voice whose silence is noticed. He is not the most seen, but the most remembered. And memory, in the attention economy, is currency.

You must also prepare for loss. Because you will fall. Every sovereign does. The crowd is mercurial. Their love is conditional. Their loyalty is brief. But you must understand falling is part of ruling. The game is not permanence. It is return. The court does not reward those who never fall. It rewards those who rise again, transformed.

Machiavelli believed that Fortuna, the goddess of chance, must be seized by the bold. Today, she is encoded in algorithms. She rewards not virtue, but velocity. Not caution, but provocation. And she does not wait. If you hesitate, another takes your place. Not with armies, but with followers.

Yet even Fortuna yields to something deeper: virtù. In Machiavelli's thought, virtù was not moral goodness, it was force of character, strategic excellence, the cultivated capacity to shape fate rather than be shaped by it. It was the soul of a ruler sharpened into will. The modern Prince must reclaim this. Not through violence, but through vision. Not through inheritance, but through design. Virtù today means narrative precision, infrastructural command, psychological fluency. It is the ability to stand not above the algorithm, but within it, and still bend the feed to your myth.

But power gained through attention is not the same as power grounded in meaning. You must never mistake engagement for influence. Likes are not loyalty. Views are not belief. You must build deeper structures. Invisible ones. Private rituals. Inner circles. Legacy channels. Because when the feed turns against you, and it will, you will need roots, not just reach.

There is a secret the old Princes knew, and that you must recover: the real power is not public. It is not in the banquet, but in the whisper. Not in the proclamation, but in the pause. The sovereign who endures is the one who learns to speak less and mean more. To vanish strategically. To appear unexpectedly. To give just enough, but never everything. The court must believe it knows you. But it must never truly have you.

And if exile comes, if you are banned, shadowed, silenced, or erased, you must remember Machiavelli in his countryside study. Disgraced, yes. Forgotten, never. Because he understood what few truly do: the story is stronger than the seat. And a Prince who masters narrative cannot be unmade.

So, when you find yourself on the edge of irrelevance, when the feed turns cold, when the crowd hungers for your ruin, do not panic. Reframe. Recast. Reappear. Write your own resurrection.

You are not the ruler of a platform. You are the architect of a myth.

And the throne? The throne is wherever your story is believed.

Now go. Write it well.

XI

Epilogue

This book began as a thesis statement to paintings that I have been creating called my Dystopian Selfies. In 2016 I started to perceive a change in the American zeitgeist. A style of art was beginning to emerge that drew upon the glitches in computer imagery. My original thesis was focused on my perspective as a serf in the middle of emerging techno-feudalism. I have included it somewhat as an epilogue to book it inspired me to write. This chapter is not for the Prince rather it is for the rest of us serfs trying to make sense of the world that has yet to fully take shape.

Dystopian Selfies and the Loneliness of the Digital Mirror

There's a moment, quiet, unspoken, that comes when scrolling through social media late at night. You see the faces: polished, curated, glowing with certainty. You see the captions: effortless wit, filtered joy, carefully aligned values. And you feel a strange ache, like looking through a pane of glass from the outside. You're supposed to feel connected, but all you feel is distance. The light from your screen reflects back not clarity, but distortion.

My Dystopian Selfies series came from that space.

They are not protests. They are not resistance. They are reflections, warped, cracked, and emotionally raw. They are what I see when I look past the filters, when I peer into the empty spaces behind the algorithmically blessed smiles. These portraits are not of specific people, but of a collective mood: the sadness, confusion, and digital disorientation that exists just beneath the surface of our curated selves.

We used to post in order to share. Now we post in order to exist. And the platforms, once neutral tools, have become stages, arenas, traps. What began as a mirror has become a hall of mirrors, and behind every reflection is the cold logic of optimization. The more we feed the machine, the less we recognize ourselves in its glow.

Economists call this era techno-feudalism. It's not just capitalism in a digital costume, it's something more ancient, more controlling. A handful of platform lords, Meta, Google, OpenAI, own the infrastructure of our emotional and social lives. They've replaced markets with fiefdoms. We don't participate; we serve. We don't share ourselves; we lease fragments of our identity to be shaped, ranked, and returned to us in the form of visibility.

But something even more uncanny is happening now. The platforms themselves are becoming populated not by people, but by simulations of people. Meta recently began rolling out AI "characters", personas trained on celebrities and influencers that exist to engage you, entertain you, and slowly blur your understanding of what's real and what isn't. The feed is no longer made by humans, it's designed by AI, filled with AI, and increasingly, performed by AI.

You log in, and you are surrounded by ghosts. The feeling sitting online among ghosts is at the core of the Dystopian Selfies. They are not a scream. They are not a manifesto. They are a quiet murmur under the noise of endless engagement. They are the feeling of uploading a real emotion into a space that can only respond with metrics. They are the slow realization that you are not connecting with others, but performing for systems. And that my audience may not even be real moving forward.

The philosopher Byung-Chul Han, in The Transparency Society, writes about this compulsion to reveal. He describes a world in which privacy, mystery, and depth are replaced by total visibility. Not because we're forced, but because we've learned to desire it. We trade opacity for attention. We give up our insides to maintain a surface. In this light, the polished profiles we see on Instagram and TikTok aren't just personal, they're political. They are proof of compliance.

But the cracks are there. If you look closely enough, you can see them, little ruptures in the flow of perfection. A face too smooth. A smile that doesn't reach the eyes. A caption that tries too hard. These are the moments I chase when painting. Not the performance, but the falter. Not the pose, but the glitch.

The glitch, to me, is the moment when the self tries to break through the persona. It's the moment when the algorithm slips and something real leaks out, sadness, exhaustion, confusion, shame. I don't paint these things to criticize the people behind the profiles. I paint them because I feel them, too. I live in this system. I am shaped by it. These portraits are not of "them", they are of us.

And yet, as the platforms evolve, that "us" feels more and more abstract. I scroll through my feed and see AI-generated models in bikinis, AI-generated influencers giving motivational speeches, AI-generated artists with tens of thousands of followers. Their images are cleaner than mine. Their messages more digestible. Their flaws perfectly simulated. They are not people, but they are rewarded like people. Often more than people.

It feels like standing in a crowd where no one is real.

The Dystopian Selfies try to hold on to that last bit of reality. The uncomfortably human. The imperfectly honest. The sadness that has no caption. The distortion that doesn't seek to impress. If the feed is a performance, these portraits are what happens when the actor walks off-stage and looks in the mirror. Not the mirror on the wall, but the broken mirror in their mind.

I don't pretend these works offer a solution. There is no way back to the internet of the early 2000s. We can't uninvent these systems, and most days, we don't want to. We are too deeply entwined. Too dependent. Too shaped. But we can name the feeling. We can hold up the distortion and say: this is happening. This is real. Even if everything around us is fake.

I paint these broken faces because I need to remember what being human feels like. Not what it looks like. Not what it performs like. But what it feels like, especially in a world that increasingly mistakes simulation for substance.

The Glitch as a Warning

We stand at the precipice of a new kind of loneliness, a digital world populated not by people, but by interactions designed to feel real without requiring human presence. The AI-influencer era is not about enhancing human creativity, it is about replacing it with something easier to control, something more predictable, something less human.

But glitch remains a signal.

A glitch in a system is an error, a crack in the seamlessness of corporate control. In Dystopian Selfies, I amplify the glitch, turning the breakdown into the subject, exposing the underlying structure of a system that seeks to erase human unpredictability. In the distortion, there is truth. In the malfunction, there is resistance.

If the future of digital engagement is artificially generated, then the role of the artist is to expose the fracture points, to force the errors, to refuse to conform to the optimization of identity.

The question is no longer "Who am I online?"

The question is: "Am I the only human left in this space?"

The Eternal Sovereign

Throughout this book, we have explored the shifting architecture of power, from the crumbling halls of the nation-state to the infinite court of the digital realm. We have named the sovereigns of our time: the algorithmic rulers, the platform architects, the code-based kings who do not wear crowns but host networks. We have drawn on Machiavelli's clarity, not as a guide to cruelty, but as a manual for survival in a world where narrative, not lineage, shapes rule.

And yet, before we leave the court, one final truth remains to be told: you are not small.

This book has spoken often of Princes, platforms, and power. But you, dear reader, may have wondered: what does this have to do with me? I do not rule. I do not build empires. I am one among billions. A name in the scroll. A face in the crowd.

But consider this: in a world increasingly ruled by networks, attention is currency. Presence is influence. And story is power. Every post, every decision, every stand you take, even if unseen by the masses, shapes the court around you. Even if that court is just your family, your community, your corner of the web.

There is no small life in a time when every life is indexed. Every action becomes part of a larger signal. What you choose to value, protect, amplify, and believe matters, not because it will be seen by millions, but because it is seen by those within your reach.

The modern Prince must master narrative to rule. But you, sovereign of your own voice, must master purpose to endure.

Your significance is not measured by scale, but by authenticity. By courage. By the way you hold your place in a shifting world without losing your shape.

So, leave this book not with despair, but with resolve.

Rule what you can.

Build what you must.

Guard your myth.

You are not small. You are sovereign.

And the court you shape, even if it is only one person deep, is real.

And it matters.

ABOUT THE AUTHOR

Kevin Eslinger is an artist and writer whose current work explores the boundaries between technology, identity, and power. With a background in fine art, toy design, and 3D visualization, his creative career spans the worlds of commercial product development, speculative archaeology, fine art painting and glitch-infused social commentary. His paintings and collectibles have been exhibited nationally.

Kevin began his career designing toys and working with companies like McFarlane Toys and Master Replicas, but over time, his focus shifted from tangible artifacts to the emotional and psychological cost of life under digital rule. In recent years, he has worked with archaeologists and researchers to visualize ancient civilizations, using 3D platforms like Unreal Engine to reconstruct lost temples and cities. His collaborations include work featured on television and in academic circles, blending history with immersive technology.

The Platform Prince began as a thesis statement for a series of glitch-art paintings called Dystopian Selfies, which reflect the fractured, hypermediated reality of modern life. These visual works, equal parts raw, surreal, and symbolic, became the seed for a book that asks not just what it means to rule in the cloud, but what it means to exist within it.

Kevin writes with the precision of a political theorist and the soul of an artist. Influenced by Machiavelli and digital culture critics, his work speaks to creators, thinkers, and anyone trying to stay human in the face of algorithmic control. He lives in Colorado with his wife and daughter, and splits his creative time between painting, writing, and virtual reconstruction.

This is his first published book

www.ingramcontent.com/pod-product-compliance
Lightning Source LLC
Chambersburg PA
CBHW020547030426
42337CB00013B/1002